iona abbey

worship book

iona abbey

worship book

The Iona Community

WILD GOOSE PUBLICATIONS
www.ionabooks.com

Contents of this volume © the individual contributors
Compilation © 2001 The Iona Community
Previous editions: *The Iona Community Worship Book*;
this new edition published 2001 by
Wild Goose Publications, Fourth Floor, Savoy House,
140 Sauchiehall St, Glasgow G51 3BA, UK
the publishing division of the Iona Community.
Scottish Charity No. SCO03794. Limited Company Reg. No. SCO96243.
web: www.ionabooks.com

1st reprint January 2002

ISBN 1 901557 50 2

Cover photograph © Larry Rasmussen

A catalogue record for this book is available from the British Library.

Distributed in Australia by
Willow Connection Pty Ltd,
Unit 4A, 3-9 Kenneth Road, Manly Vale, NSW 2093, Australia

and in New Zealand by
Pleroma Christian Supplies,
Higginson St., Otane 4170, Central Hawkes Bay, New Zealand

Permission to reproduce any part of this work in Australia
or New Zealand should be sought from Willow Connection.

Printed by Bell & Bain, Glasgow, UK

CONTENTS

Other Services:

PREFACE

Work and worship are inseparable. Both were needed to bring this book into being. Every few years the Iona Community undertakes the revision of this resource, used daily in the Abbey, so that it continues to reflect the growth and creative changes in our life and worship. This edition is the culmination of two years of discussion, trial, re-drafting and theological debate by members of the resident group on the island, in relationship with the Wild Goose Resource Group and in consultation with the wider membership of the Iona Community. The words and thoughts of countless people – staff, members and visiting friends – are to be found in these pages, or have contributed towards the form in which it now appears. It cannot be called the *final* form: as we hand it to the publishers new suggestions are still emerging, which must await the *next* revision! What you have in your hands is provisional, and must always be. It has evolved in a way that is consistent with the very nature of worship – as a dynamic process based on relationship, seeking to find words for that which words cannot express. These liturgies can never be a finished product, therefore. They must point beyond themselves, opening doors to bring people together and windows to set them free.

What is new in this book? Two services in their entirety. A Leaving Service, based on the morning office, with its focus on travelling on; and an Agape in recognition of the moments when the Abbey's open Communion Table can still divide the very people it is meant to unite. Changes to the morning order include the appearance of an Affirmation, and the removal of the morning songs to the General Worship Resources at the back – to be joined there by a selection of evening songs and a few others. The appendices, which were so usefully created ten years ago with additional material for many specific acts of worship, are no longer at the back, but immediately follow the relevant service as 'extra resources'. The most expanded of these is the section following Afternoon Prayers for Justice and Peace, in which we offer more alternatives while no longer tying specific themes to particular days.

Perhaps this pinpoints one of our aims – to provide more tools and options, with usefulness and flexibility in mind.

Finally (because they come at the very end of the book) the Psalms for morning worship. Determined to find the most straightforward and inclusive translation, we have ended up writing our own. We cannot pretend we were translating from the Hebrew, but we hope that we have retained something of the Hebraic poetry, flow and directness.

This is a book for the Abbey and all who worship in it; but in all the changes we have made we have been mindful of its wider use. We are glad to know that its liturgies and resources are well used and adapted world-wide. Long may it be so. Other songs, chants and liturgies can be obtained from the *Wild Goose Resource Group* and *Wild Goose Publications* in Glasgow. The Iona Community itself exists to be of service to the whole church and the world beyond the church, as we seek new ways to touch the hearts of all. If we have something of value here, we would not want to confine it to Iona. From the time of Saint Columba, that has never been the intention. It is in the common life, wherever we are, that community is to be rebuilt, Christ celebrated and prayer offered by ordinary people in honest and relevant language. Books like this seem to help, and for that we give thanks.

Iona Abbey
Advent, 2000

THE IONA COMMUNITY

The Iona Community is an ecumenical Christian community that is committed to seeking new ways of living the Gospel in today's world. It was founded in 1938 by the Revd George MacLeod, when he was a parish minister in Glasgow. Initially its purpose was expressed through the rebuilding of the monastic quarters of the mediaeval abbey on Iona, and pursued in mission and ministry throughout Scotland and beyond. The Community remains committed to rebuilding the common life through working for social and political change, striving for the renewal of the church with an ecumenical emphasis, and exploring new, more inclusive approaches to worship.

The Community now has over 240 Members, about 1500 Associate Members and around 1500 Friends. The Members – women and men, lay and ordained, from many backgrounds and different church traditions, living throughout Britain with a few overseas – are committed to a five-fold Rule involving a daily devotional discipline, sharing and accounting for their use of time and money, regular meeting, and action for justice and peace. A number of concerns have been identified as particular priorities:

- the promotion of justice and peace, through, for example:
    - opposing nuclear weapons and seeking reduction in the arms trade,
    - supporting the cause of the poor and the exploited in Britain and abroad,
    - political activity in combating racism,
    - engagement with environmental and constitutional issues;
- the exploration of human sexuality;
- commitment to strengthening understanding between church traditions, and to the sharing of communion;
- concern for young people;
- the promotion of inter-faith dialogue;

- the rediscovery of an approach to spirituality appropriate to our times;
- the development of the ministry of healing.

At the Community's three residential centres – the Abbey and the MacLeod Centre on Iona, and Camas Outdoor Centre on the Ross of Mull – guests are welcomed during the season that runs from March to October, and over Christmas. The centres are run by a resident group of about 25 people, including several Community members, assisted by around 30 volunteers from all over the world. Hospitality is provided for over 110 people in all (45 in the Abbey, 50 in the MacLeod Centre; up to 20 at Camas), along with a unique opportunity to extend horizons and forge new relationships by sharing with staff and other guests an experience of the common life in worship, work, discussion and relaxation. This is usually through week-long programmes which often focus on themes relating to the concerns of the Community. The Community's shop on Iona, just outside the Abbey grounds, carries an attractive range of books and craft goods.

The Community's administrative headquarters are in Glasgow, which also serves as a base for work with young people, the Wild Goose Resource Group working in the field of worship, a bi-monthly magazine, *Coracle*, and a publishing house, Wild Goose Publications. Between Glasgow and Iona the Community now has a staff of almost fifty people.

For information contact:
The Iona Community, Fourth Floor, Savoy House
140 Sauchiehall Street, Glasgow G2 3DH, UK
(phone: 0141 332 6343; e-mail: ionacomm@gla.iona.org.uk).

For enquiries about visiting Iona, please contact:
Iona Abbey, Isle of Iona, Argyll, PA76 6SN
(phone: 01681 700404; e-mail: ionacomm@iona.org.uk).

CONCERNING WORSHIP

The services in this book reflect important aspects of what the Iona Community believes about worship.

We owe our very existence as a community to the central Gospel conviction that worship is all that we are and all that we do. Either everything we do is an offering to God, or nothing. We may not pick and choose.

Our whole life, we believe, is a search for wholeness. We desire to be fully human, with no division into the 'sacred' and the 'secular'. We desire to be fully present to God, who is fully present to us, whether in our neighbour or in the political and social activity of the world around us, whether in the field of culture or of economics, and whether in prayer and praise together or in the very centre and soul of our being.

Of ourselves we cannot make this happen. We cannot make ourselves whole any more than we can make ourselves happy or good. But we do believe that by grace we are to structure our lives, both individually and together, in obedience to the vision that God has given us of what wholeness is like, primarily through the life, death and resurrection of Jesus Christ.

So, on Iona, we are committed to the belief that worship is everything we do, both inside and outside the church. We begin each day with prayer together, common prayer, for we are a community, given to each other by God. In the morning service we do not end with a benediction, but simply with responses that prepare us to go straight out to the life of the world, there to continue worship in the context of our work. In the evening we come together again for common prayer, but we do not begin the service with a call to worship, for we have been at worship all day long. And only in the evening service do we have a final benediction at the close of the day.

In this symbolic way we try to express our conviction that the whole of our day is all of a piece, bracketed with common prayer, but continuing throughout every action of work , common life and recreation as one liturgy, one work of service offered to God.

On Iona, our common life is fed from many sources. The past is all around us. We are the inheritors of the Celtic tradition, with its deep sense of Jesus as the head of all, and of God's glory in all of creation. So we use prayers from the Celtic Church for welcome, for work, and in expressing the needs of the world. We are the inheritors of the Benedictine tradition, with its conviction that 'to work is to pray', its commitment to hospitality, and its sense of order, all reflected in our services and our lifestyle. And we are the inheritors of the tradition of the Reformers, with their evangelical zeal, their call to commitment, and their deep understanding of the continuing challenge to every generation to find 'new ways to touch the hearts of all'. All this, we hope, you will find in how we pray and work on Iona.

Because we are an ecumenical community, we also draw on many modern Christian traditions in our services. This is a great privilege for us, and something we value very highly. It also reminds us that our life and our services here are no 'hole in the corner' affair. All we are and all we do, our work and our prayer, are part of the ongoing prayer and work of the whole Church in heaven and on earth: we are part of the one communion of saints.

A time on Iona often changes people. God has clearly used this place very powerfully over the centuries. The Iona Community does not believe that we are brought here to be changed into 'religious' people, but rather to be made more fully human. Our common life, including our services, is directed to that end.

In the words of the German martyr Dietrich Bonhoeffer, we believe that 'the Christian is not a religious person, but simply a human being, as Jesus was a human being, profoundly this-worldly, characterised by discipline, and the constant knowledge of death and resurrection'.

THE MORNING SERVICE

Opening responses

4.12.15

Leader: The world belongs to God,

ALL: THE EARTH AND ALL ITS PEOPLE.

Leader: How good it is, how wonderful,

ALL: TO LIVE TOGETHER IN UNITY.

Leader: Love and faith come together,

ALL: JUSTICE AND PEACE JOIN HANDS.

Leader: If Christ's disciples keep silent

ALL: THESE STONES WOULD SHOUT ALOUD.

Leader: Open our lips, O God,

ALL: AND OUR MOUTHS SHALL PROCLAIM YOUR PRAISE.

Morning song of praise

Confession

4.12.15

Leader: Holy God, Maker of all

ALL: HAVE MERCY ON US.

Leader: Jesus Christ, Servant of the poor

ALL: HAVE MERCY ON US.

Leader: Holy Spirit, Breath of life

ALL: HAVE MERCY ON US

(Here the leader may offer a brief prayer of confession)

Leader:	Let us in silence confess our faults and admit our frailty.

Silence

4. 12. 15

Leader: Before God, with the people of God,

I confess to my brokenness:

to the ways I wound my life,

the lives of others,

and the life of the world.

ALL: MAY GOD FORGIVE YOU, CHRIST RENEW YOU,

AND THE SPIRIT ENABLE YOU TO GROW IN LOVE.

Leader: Amen.

ALL: BEFORE GOD, WITH THE PEOPLE OF GOD,

WE CONFESS TO OUR BROKENNESS:

TO THE WAYS WE WOUND OUR LIVES,

THE LIVES OF OTHERS,

AND THE LIFE OF THE WORLD.

Leader: May God forgive you, Christ renew you,

and the Spirit enable you to grow in love.

ALL: AMEN.

Prayer for God's help

Leader: Move among us, O God; give us life:

ALL: LET YOUR PEOPLE REJOICE IN YOU.

Leader: Make our hearts clean within us:

ALL: RENEW US IN MIND AND IN SPIRIT.

Leader: Give us again the joy of your help:

ALL: WITH YOUR SPIRIT OF FREEDOM SUSTAIN US.

(Here the leader may offer a brief prayer for God's help)

Leader: And now, as Jesus taught us, we say:

ALL: OUR FATHER IN HEAVEN,

               HALLOWED BE YOUR NAME,

               YOUR KINGDOM COME,

               YOUR WILL BE DONE ON EARTH AS IN HEAVEN,

               GIVE US TODAY OUR DAILY BREAD,

               FORGIVE US OUR SINS

               AS WE FORGIVE THOSE WHO SIN AGAINST US,

               SAVE US IN THE TIME OF TRIAL

               AND DELIVER US FROM EVIL,

               FOR THE KINGDOM, THE POWER

               AND THE GLORY ARE YOURS,

               NOW AND FOR EVER. AMEN.

Affirmation

Leader: With the whole church

ALL: WE AFFIRM

               THAT WE ARE MADE IN GOD'S IMAGE,

               BEFRIENDED BY CHRIST, EMPOWERED BY THE SPIRIT.

Leader: With people everywhere

ALL: WE AFFIRM

               GOD'S GOODNESS AT THE HEART OF HUMANITY,

               PLANTED MORE DEEPLY THAN ALL THAT IS WRONG.

Leader: With all creation

ALL: WE CELEBRATE

THE MIRACLE AND WONDER OF LIFE;

THE UNFOLDING PURPOSES OF GOD,

FOREVER AT WORK IN OURSELVES AND THE WORLD.

Psalm   *(said responsively)*

The reading for the day

Leader: This morning's reading comes from …

Listen now for the Word of God.

Reading   *(After the reading, there is a period of silence,*

at the end of which the leader says)

Leader: For the Word of God in scripture,

for the Word of God among us,

for the Word of God within us

ALL: THANKS BE TO GOD.

Song

Prayers of gratitude and concern

(Here the leader may offer a short prayer of thanksgiving,

followed by prayers for:

–   the needs of the world and the life of the church

–   concerns of the Iona Community

–   members of the Iona Community and their families.

Between these prayers, the response is:)

Leader:	God, in your mercy,
ALL:	HEAR OUR PRAYER.

(The prayer for Community members ends with:)

Leader:	Living God, may they not fail you,
ALL:	NOR WE FAIL THEM.

(Then the leader says one of the following prayers:)

Monday   O God,
lead us from death to life, from falsehood to truth.
Lead us from despair to hope, from fear to trust.
Lead us from hate to love, from war to peace.
Let peace fill our hearts, our world, our universe.
We ask it for your own name's sake.
AMEN.

Tuesday   O Christ, the Master Carpenter,
who at the last, through wood and nails,
purchased our whole salvation,
wield well your tools in the workshop of your world,
so that we who come rough-hewn to your bench
may here be fashioned to a truer beauty of your hand.
We ask it for your own name's sake.
AMEN.

Wednesday   O God, who gave to your servant Columba
the gifts of courage, faith and cheerfulness,
and sent people forth from Iona

to carry the word of your gospel to every creature:

grant, we pray, a like spirit to your church,

even at this present time.

Further in all things the purpose of our community,

that hidden things may be revealed to us,

and new ways found to touch the hearts of all.

May we preserve with each other

sincere charity and peace,

and, if it be your holy will,

grant that this place of your abiding be continued still

to be a sanctuary and a light.

Through Jesus Christ.

AMEN.

Thursday   O God, you have set before us a great hope

that your kingdom will come on earth,

and have taught us to pray for its coming:

make us ready to thank you for the signs of its dawning,

and to pray and work for the perfect day

when your will shall be done on earth as it is in heaven.

In the name of Jesus Christ.

AMEN.

Friday   O Christ, you are within each of us.

It is not just the interior of these walls:

it is our own inner being you have renewed.

We are your temple not made with hands.

We are your body.

If every wall should crumble, and every church decay,

we are your habitation.

Nearer are you than breathing,

closer than hands and feet.

Ours are the eyes with which you, in the mystery,

look out with compassion on the world.

Yet we bless you for this place,

for your directing of us, your redeeming of us,

and your indwelling.

Take us outside, O Christ, outside holiness,

out to where soldiers curse and nations clash

at the crossroads of the world.

So shall this building continue to be justified.

We ask it for your own name's sake.

AMEN.

Saturday O God, set your blessing on us

as we begin this day together.

Confirm us in the truth by which we rightly live;

confront us with the truth from which we wrongly turn.

We ask not for what we want,

but for what you know we need,

as we offer this day and ourselves for you and to you,

through Jesus Christ, our Saviour.

AMEN.

Silence

Closing responses *(All standing in preparation to leave)*

Leader   This is the day that God has made;

ALL: WE WILL REJOICE AND BE GLAD IN IT.

Leader: We will not offer to God

ALL: OFFERINGS THAT COST US NOTHING.

Leader: Go in peace to love and to serve;

ALL: WE WILL SEEK PEACE AND PURSUE IT.

Leader: In the name of the Trinity of Love,

ALL: GOD IN COMMUNITY, HOLY AND ONE.

(We remain standing to leave, the work of our day flowing directly from our worship)

THE LEAVING SERVICE

Opening responses

Leader: The world belongs to God,

ALL: THE EARTH AND ALL ITS PEOPLE.

Leader: How good it is, how wonderful,

ALL: TO LIVE TOGETHER IN UNITY.

Leader: Love and faith come together,

ALL: JUSTICE AND PEACE JOIN HANDS.

Leader: If Christ's disciples keep silent

ALL: THESE STONES WOULD SHOUT ALOUD.

Leader: Open our lips, O God,

ALL: AND OUR MOUTHS SHALL PROCLAIM YOUR PRAISE.

Morning song of praise

Prayer of confession

Leader: Holy God, Maker of all

ALL: HAVE MERCY ON US.

Leader: Jesus Christ, Servant of the poor

ALL: HAVE MERCY ON US.

Leader: Holy Spirit, Breath of life

ALL: HAVE MERCY ON US

(Here the leader may offer a brief prayer of confession)

Leader: Let us in silence confess our faults and admit our frailty.

Silence

Leader: Before God, with the people of God,

I confess to my brokenness:

to the ways I wound my life,

the lives of others,

and the life of the world.

ALL: MAY GOD FORGIVE YOU, CHRIST RENEW YOU,

AND THE SPIRIT ENABLE YOU TO GROW IN LOVE.

Leader: Amen.

ALL: BEFORE GOD, WITH THE PEOPLE OF GOD,

WE CONFESS TO OUR BROKENNESS:

TO THE WAYS WE WOUND OUR LIVES,

THE LIVES OF OTHERS,

AND THE LIFE OF THE WORLD.

Leader: May God forgive you, Christ renew you,

and the Spirit enable you to grow in love.

ALL: AMEN.

The letting go

Leader: As Columba laid down his books

and the security of the monastery,

ALL: SO WE LAY DOWN WHAT IS PAST

AND LOOK TO THE FUTURE.

Leader: As Brigid, with a cross of rushes,

comforted a stranger,

ALL: SO WE TAKE INTO DAILY LIFE

SIGNS OF HOPE AND HEALING.

Leader: As Patrick travelled ever on,

as Margaret built community,

ALL: SO WE REACH BEYOND OURSELVES,

TO SHARE THE LIVES OF OTHERS

AND TOUCH A WIDER WORLD.

Leader: And as Jesus taught us, so we say:

ALL: OUR FATHER IN HEAVEN,

HALLOWED BE YOUR NAME,

YOUR KINGDOM COME,

YOUR WILL BE DONE ON EARTH AS IN HEAVEN,

GIVE US TODAY OUR DAILY BREAD,

FORGIVE US OUR SINS

AS WE FORGIVE THOSE WHO SIN AGAINST US,

SAVE US IN THE TIME OF TRIAL

AND DELIVER US FROM EVIL,

FOR THE KINGDOM, THE POWER

AND THE GLORY ARE YOURS,

NOW AND FOR EVER.

AMEN.

A psalm for sending *(said responsively)*

The reading for the day

Leader: This morning's reading comes from …

Listen now for the word of God.

Reading   *(After the reading, there is a period of silence, at the end of*

which the leader says)

Leader: For the Word of God in scripture,

for the Word of God among us,

for the Word of God within us

ALL: THANKS BE TO GOD.

Song

Prayers of gratitude and concern

Either: *The leader invites people to call out things from their time*

on Iona for which they wish to give thanks.

or: *The following litany of thanksgiving may be used:*

Leader: For the roots of our Community,

and of *all* our communities:

ALL: WE THANK YOU, LIVING GOD.

Leader: For what we share together here,

and for the life we share with others:

ALL: WE THANK YOU, LIVING GOD.

Leader: For the path that lies before us now,

and our futures in your hands:

ALL: WE THANK YOU, LIVING GOD.

(Then the leader offers prayers for:

–   *the needs of the world and the life of the church*

–   *concerns of the Iona Community*

–   *members of the Iona Community and their families.*

Between these prayers, the response is:)

Leader:	God, in your mercy,
ALL:	HEAR OUR PRAYER.

(The prayer for Community members ends with:)

Leader:	Living God, may they not fail you,
ALL:	NOR WE FAIL THEM

(This is followed by the prayer for Friday):

Leader: O Christ, you are within each of us.

It is not just the interior of these walls:

it is our own inner being you have renewed.

We are your temple not made with hands.

We are your body.

If every wall should crumble, and every church decay,

we are your habitation.

Nearer are you than breathing,

closer than hands and feet.

Ours are the eyes with which you, in the mystery,

look out with compassion on the world.

Yet we bless you for this place,

for your directing of us, your redeeming of us,

and your indwelling.

Take us outside, O Christ, outside holiness,

out to where soldiers curse and nations clash

at the crossroads of the world.

So shall this building continue to be justified.

We ask it for your own name's sake. AMEN.

Silence

Parting blessing *(All standing in preparation to leave)*

Either – this reciprocal blessing:

Leader, with all who are staying:

The Maker's blessing be yours

on your road

on your journey

guiding you, cherishing you.

All who are leaving today:

The Son's blessing be yours

wine and water

bread and stories

feeding you, challenging you.

Leader, with those staying:

The Spirit's blessing be yours

wind and fire

joy and wisdom

comforting you, disturbing you.

Those leaving:

The Angels' blessing be yours

on your house

on your living

guarding you, encouraging you.

ALL: GOD'S BLESSING BE OURS;

THE BLESSING OF PILGRIMS

ALL THE NIGHTS AND DAYS

OF OUR JOURNEY HOME.

Or – *the following:*

Leader: May God, who is present in sunrise and nightfall,

and in the crossing of the sea,

guide your feet as you go.

May God, who is with you when you sit

and when you stand,

encompass you with love

and lead you by the hand.

May God, who knows your path

and the places where you rest,

be with you in your waiting,

be your good news for sharing,

and lead you in the way that is everlasting.

ALL: AMEN.

(We remain standing to leave, our work or travel flowing

directly from our worship)

CONCERNING THE CELEBRATION OF COMMUNION

We celebrate Communion twice weekly in the Abbey Church, on Sunday morning and on the evening before the guests leave. Because we are an ecumenical community, we bring a wide range of traditions to this celebration. Some call it the Lord's Supper or the Holy Communion, while others refer to it as the Eucharist, the Mass or the Breaking of Bread. We believe that the invitation to this sacrament comes not from any church or individual, but from Jesus. We therefore invite in Christ's name all who hear his invitation and who wish to respond by receiving the bread and the wine. If for any reason people do not wish to receive the elements as they are distributed from hand to hand throughout the church, we suggest that they simply pass the bread and the wine from their neighbour on one side to their neighbour on the other, and remain united with us in prayer.

On Sunday morning, when the Abbey Church is often filled with visitors and pilgrims from around the world, our service is a structured liturgy of celebrating the sacrament of Christ's Presence. When we sit together at the end of our week, around the long table set up in the Abbey Church, our evening service is a more intimate sharing of the Bread of Life, as well as being a festive looking-forward to the Kingdom of God when men and women will come from east and west, north and south, to sit at table together. Both services follow the four-fold action of Jesus at the last supper, when he took bread, blessed it, broke the bread and shared it and the wine.

Jesus took the bread and the wine. After the Word of God has been proclaimed the first action of our liturgy of communion is, in response, to offer the wine and the bread, baked in the kitchen of the Abbey or MacLeod Centre. The elements are signs of the body of Jesus and of his self-giving, and are also signs of our offering. The bread and wine which we offer as gifts of the earth and work of human hands also represent our bodies, our lives which again we offer to God. As St Augustine said to his people when they had placed the elements on the altar, 'There you are upon the table, there you are in the cup.'

Jesus blessed the bread and the wine. Just as Jesus was blessed with God's Spirit, so we, having offered ourselves, seek a blessing upon our lives and on the bread and wine; we seek a renewing of the life of Christ in us. It is a 're-membering' or 're-bodying' of Christ. It is over our lives as well as over the bread and wine that the words of blessing are spoken. As St Chrysostom said, through the blessed food and drink we are renewed as 'flesh of Christ's flesh, and bone of Christ's bone'.

Jesus broke the bread and poured out the wine. In breaking the bread we remember the brokenness of Jesus' body on the cross and commit ourselves to travelling the path of sacrificial love. Jesus' words at the Last Supper – 'Do this' – challenge us not merely to break bread together but to open ourselves to the cost of discipleship. St Paul wrote to the early Christians in Rome, 'Present your bodies as a living sacrifice.' Just as on the road to Emmaus it was in the breaking of bread that the risen Christ was known to his disciples (Luke 24), so in the self-giving of our lives is Christ known to the world today.

Jesus shared the bread and the wine. During the distribution of the bread and wine we remember Jesus sharing his life with the disciples and with the poor and sick, and we are called to a sharing of our own lives and possessions with one another and the poor. The final blessing of the service returns us to where we began. As we begin by bringing all that we are into communion, so we end by taking our renewed selves back into the details of our common life. We follow the bread and wine out of church, and whether on a Sunday morning in the cloisters or on a Thursday evening in the refectory we continue our celebration of communion out in the place of the ordinary. And in sharing ourselves with one another we share Christ.

SUNDAY MORNING COMMUNION

Opening responses:

Leader: Thanks be to you, O God, that we have risen this day,

ALL: TO THE RISING OF THIS LIFE ITSELF.

Leader: Be the purpose of God between us and each purpose,

ALL: THE HAND OF GOD BETWEEN US AND EACH HAND,

Leader: The pain of Christ between us and each pain,

ALL: THE LOVE OF CHRIST BETWEEN US AND EACH LOVE.

Leader: O God, who brought us to the bright light

of this new day

ALL: BRING US TO THE GUIDING LIGHT OF ETERNITY.

Or: **Alternative responses:**

(holy)

Leader: Welcome to this ancient place:

11.12.2006
4.19.15

ALL: HOUSE OF PRAYER FOR MANY NATIONS;

HOME TO ALL WHO COME.

Leader: Welcome to this gathering place:

ALL: FRIEND AND STRANGER, SAINT AND SINNER

IN ALL WHO GATHER HERE.

(to)

Leader: Come with hope or hesitation;

come with joy or yearning;

all who hunger, all who thirst

for life in all its fullness.

ALL: GENEROUS GOD AND GENEROUS SAVIOUR,

TOUCH US THROUGH YOUR SPIRIT.

Song

Jesus calls us

1. Jesus calls us here to meet him
    as, through word and song and prayer,
    we affirm God's promised presence,
    where his people live and care,
    praise the God who keeps his promise,
    praise the Son who calls us friends,
    praise the Spirit who, among us,
    to our hopes and fears attends.

2. Jesus calls us to confess him
    Word of Life and Lord of All,
    sharer of our flesh and frailness,
    saving all who fail and fall.
    Tell his holy human story,
    tell his tales that all may hear,
    tell the world that Christ in glory
    came to earth to meet us here.

3. Jesus calls us to each other:
    found in him are no divides.
    Race and class and sex and language,
    such are barriers he derides.
    Join the hands of friend and stranger,
    join the hands of age and youth,
    join the faithful and the doubter
    in their common search for truth.

4.   Jesus calls us to his table,
      rooted firm in time and space,
      where the church in earth and heaven
      finds a common meeting place.
      Share the bread and wine, his body,
      share the love of which we sing,
      share the feast for saints and sinners,
      hosted by our Lord and King.

Or: **Women and men as God intended**

1.   Women and men as God intended,

4. 19. 15

      daughters of Adam, sons of Eve;
      children of earth, loved by their Maker,
      those only heaven could conceive;
      yet in our loving we are not one
      with heaven's deep intent:
      we are not as God meant.

2.   Ours is the shame, ours is the story,
      ours is a squandered legacy;
      fallen from grace, fearful of glory,
      lost is our true humanity.
      How can the goodness heaven endowed
      which earth cannot afford
      be once again restored?

3.   Into our world, born of a woman

4. 19. 18

      comes, in the flesh, the living God;

Moved by our plight, suffering rejection,

feeling for those whose lives are flawed,

pardoning all who truly repent

comes Jesus Christ our Lord,

God's liberating Word.

4. Now sing aloud! Jesus our brother

turns every tide of history,

sharing our flesh, bearing our sorrow,

winning an endless liberty.

Out of the grave, alive in the world,

Christ wills all be made new;

this tested Word is true.

Or: **'Come, Host of heaven'**

1. Come, Host of heaven's high dwelling place,

come, earth's disputed guest,

find in this house a welcome home,

stay here and take your rest.

2. Surround these walls with faith and love,

that through the nights and days,

when human tongues from speaking cease,

these stones may echo praise.

3. Bless and inspire those gathered here

with patience, hope and peace,

and all the joys that know the depth

in which all sorrows cease.

4.   Here may the losers find their worth,
        the strangers find a friend,
        here may the hopeless find their faith
        and aimless find an end.

5.   Build from the human fabric signs
        of how your kingdom thrives;
        of how the Holy Spirit changes life
        through changing lives.

6.   So to the Lord whose care enfolds
        the world held in his hands
        be glory, honour, love and praise
        for which this house now stands.

Call to prayer

Leader: We gather in God's name.

ALL: WE CLAIM CHRIST'S PROMISED PRESENCE.

Leader: My brothers and sisters,
                not out of dread and fear,
                but believing that God is faithful to forgive,
                let us rid ourselves of what we need to carry no longer.

                (All sit or kneel)

Prayer of Confession and Restoration

Spoken response:

Leader: Holy God,

ALL:　　　　HOLY AND MIGHTY,

　　　　　　　HOLY AND IMMORTAL,

　　　　　　　HAVE MERCY ON US.

Or: *Sung response:*

Kyrie Eleison	Lord, have mercy
Christe Eleison	Christ, have mercy
Kyrie Eleison	Lord, have mercy.

Reading

When the reading is not the Gospel it is introduced as follows:

Leader:　　Let us prepare ourselves for the Word of God

　　　　　　as it comes to us in the reading of Holy Scripture.

ALL:　　　OUR HEARTS AND MINDS ARE OPEN.

Reader:　　A reading from …

　　　　　　(after the reading there is a period of silence,

　　　　　　at the end of which the reader says …)

Reader:　　This is the Word of God.

ALL:　　　THANKS BE TO GOD.

When the reading for the day is the Gospel, it may be introduced as follows:

Leader:　　Let us greet the Gospel of Christ

　　　　　　by standing to sing Alleluia.

　　　　　　(after the Alleluia, remain standing for the reading

　　　　　　of the Gospel)

Reader:　　A reading from …

*(after the reading, there is a period of silence, at the end of which **either** the Alleluia is sung again, **or** the following response is said …)*

Reader: This is the Gospel of Christ.

ALL: PRAISE TO CHRIST OUR LORD.

Song

(during the last verse of which children may leave for the Chapter House)

Sermon

An affirmation of faith   *(The people standing)*

ALL: WE BELIEVE IN GOD ABOVE US,

MAKER AND SUSTAINER OF ALL LIFE,

OF SUN AND MOON,

OF WATER AND EARTH,

OF MALE AND FEMALE.

WE BELIEVE IN GOD BESIDE US,

JESUS CHRIST, THE WORD MADE FLESH,

BORN OF A WOMAN, SERVANT OF THE POOR,

TORTURED AND NAILED TO A TREE.

A MAN OF SORROWS, HE DIED FORSAKEN.

HE DESCENDED INTO THE EARTH

TO THE PLACE OF DEATH.

ON THE THIRD DAY HE ROSE FROM THE TOMB.

HE ASCENDED INTO HEAVEN

TO BE EVERYWHERE PRESENT,

AND HIS KINGDOM WILL COME ON EARTH.

WE BELIEVE IN GOD WITHIN US,

THE HOLY SPIRIT OF PENTECOSTAL FIRE,

LIFE-GIVING BREATH OF THE CHURCH,

SPIRIT OF HEALING AND FORGIVENESS,

SOURCE OF RESURRECTION AND OF ETERNAL LIFE.

AMEN.

Or: **The Apostles' Creed**

ALL: WE BELIEVE IN GOD, THE FATHER ALMIGHTY,

CREATOR OF HEAVEN AND EARTH.

WE BELIEVE IN JESUS CHRIST, HIS ONLY SON, OUR LORD,

WHO WAS CONCEIVED BY THE POWER

OF THE HOLY SPIRIT

AND BORN OF THE VIRGIN MARY.

HE SUFFERED UNDER PONTIUS PILATE,

WAS CRUCIFIED, DIED AND WAS BURIED.

HE DESCENDED TO THE DEAD.

ON THE THIRD DAY HE ROSE AGAIN.

HE ASCENDED INTO HEAVEN

AND IS SEATED AT THE RIGHT HAND OF THE FATHER.

HE WILL COME AGAIN TO JUDGE THE LIVING

AND THE DEAD.

WE BELIEVE IN THE HOLY SPIRIT,

THE HOLY CATHOLIC CHURCH,

THE COMMUNION OF SAINTS,

THE FORGIVENESS OF SINS,

THE RESURRECTION OF THE BODY,

AND THE LIFE EVERLASTING. AMEN.

Prayers of intercession

(ending with the Lord's Prayer:)

ALL: OUR FATHER IN HEAVEN,
HALLOWED BE YOUR NAME,
YOUR KINGDOM COME,
YOUR WILL BE DONE ON EARTH AS IN HEAVEN,
GIVE US TODAY OUR DAILY BREAD,
FORGIVE US OUR SINS
AS WE FORGIVE THOSE WHO SIN AGAINST US,
SAVE US IN THE TIME OF TRIAL
AND DELIVER US FROM EVIL,
FOR THE KINGDOM, THE POWER
AND THE GLORY ARE YOURS,
NOW AND FOR EVER.
AMEN.

Offering

Invitation

Communion song

The hand of heaven

1.   We, who live by sound and symbol,
we, who learn from sight and word,
find these married in the person
of the one we call our Lord.
Taking bread to be his body,
taking wine to be his blood,

he let thought take flesh in action,

he let faith take root in food.

2. Not just once with special people

not just hidden deep in time,

but, wherever Christ is followed,

earthly fare becomes sublime.

Though to sound this seems a mystery,

though to sense it seems absurd,

yet in faith, which seems like folly,

we meet Jesus Christ our Lord.

3. God, our Maker, send your Spirit

to pervade the bread we break.

Let it bring the life we long for

and the love which we forsake.

Bind us closer to each other,

both forgiving and forgiven;

give us grace in this and all things

to discern the hand of heaven.

Or: **Come, Lord, be our guest**

1. Come, Lord, be our guest

find your way among us;

you whose word and will

sowed the seed which sprung us.

Earth your former home,

still is where we meet you;

therefore we greet you,

Christ, our God alone.

2.   Come, Lord, be our guest
      join our conversation;
      free our tongues to speak
      without reservation.
      Where your people meet,
      you perfect their pleasure;
      therefore we treasure
      all you have to share.

3.   Come, Lord, be our guest.
      Gathered round your table,
      we confess our faith
      more than fact or fable.
      You who made, of old,
      all that earth was needing,
      blessing and feeding
      here will make us new.

4.   Come, Lord, be our host,
      bread and wine are waiting.
      On your words depend
      all our celebrating.
      Fill us with your love,
      healing and forgiving;
      then, in us living,
      show our love your way.

Or: **Among us and before us, Lord, you stand**

1. Among us and before us, Lord, you stand
   with arms outstretched and bread and wine at hand.
   Confronting those unworthy of a crumb,
   you ask that to your table we should come.

2. Who dare say No, when such is your resolve
   our worst to witness, suffer and absolve,
   our best to raise in lives by God forgiven,
   our souls to fill on earth with food from heaven?

3. Who dare say No, when such is your intent
   to love the selves we famish and resent,
   to cradle our uncertainties and fear,
   to kindle hope as you in faith draw near?

4. Who dare say No, when such is your request
   that each around your table should be guest,
   that here the ancient word should live as new
   Take, eat and drink – all this is meant for you?

5. No more we hesitate and wonder why;
   no more we stand indifferent, scared or shy.
   Your invitation leads us to say Yes,
   to meet you where you nourish, heal and bless.

The Story of the Last Supper

(All remain standing as the story is told, then sit or kneel for the prayer)

Celebrant: Let us pray:

ALL: LOVING GOD,

THROUGH YOUR GOODNESS

WE HAVE THIS BREAD AND WINE TO OFFER,

WHICH EARTH HAS GIVEN

AND HUMAN HANDS HAVE MADE.

MAY WE KNOW YOUR PRESENCE

IN THE SHARING OF THIS BREAD,

SO THAT WE MAY KNOW YOUR TOUCH

IN ALL BREAD, ALL MATTER.

WE CELEBRATE THE LIFE THAT JESUS HAS SHARED

AMONG HIS COMMUNITY THROUGH THE CENTURIES,

AND SHARES WITH US NOW.

MADE ONE IN CHRIST

AND ONE WITH EACH OTHER,

WE OFFER THESE GIFTS AND WITH THEM OURSELVES,

A SINGLE, HOLY, LIVING SACRIFICE.

AMEN.

The Thanksgiving

Celebrant: The Lord be with you,

ALL: AND ALSO WITH YOU.

Celebrant: Lift up your hearts,

ALL: WE LIFT THEM UP TO GOD.

Celebrant: Let us give thanks to God,

ALL: IT IS RIGHT TO GIVE BOTH THANKS AND PRAISE.

Sanctus and Benedictus

ALL: HOLY, HOLY, HOLY LORD, GOD OF POWER AND MIGHT,

HEAVEN AND EARTH ARE FULL OF YOUR GLORY,

HOSANNA IN THE HIGHEST.

BLESSED IS THE ONE WHO COMES

IN THE NAME OF THE LORD.

HOSANNA IN THE HIGHEST.

Prayer of Consecration

The Communion:

Agnus Dei

Lamb of God, you take away the sin of the world.

Have mercy on us.

Lamb of God, you take away the sin of the world.

Have mercy on us.

Lamb of God, you take away the sin of the world.

Grant us your peace.

Or:

Agnus Dei, qui tollis peccata mundi, miserere nobis.

Agnus Dei, qui tollis peccata mundi, miserere nobis.

Agnus Dei, qui tollis peccata mundi, dona nobis pacem.

(We share communion by serving one another. Some will say, as they pass the bread and cup to their neighbour: 'The body of Christ' and 'The blood of Christ'; and respond as they receive it: 'Amen.')

Prayer after Communion

Sharing of the Peace   *(All stand)*

Celebrant: May the peace of Christ be with you.

ALL: AND ALSO WITH YOU.

(We offer one another a sign of the peace of Christ)

Blessing

Celebrant: May the everlasting God shield you,

               east and west and wherever you go.

               And the blessing of God be upon you.

ALL: THE BLESSING OF THE GOD OF LIFE.

Celebrant: The blessing of Christ be upon you,

ALL: THE BLESSING OF THE CHRIST OF LOVE.

Celebrant: The blessing of the Spirit be upon you,

ALL: THE BLESSING OF THE SPIRIT OF GRACE.

Celebrant: The blessing of the Trinity be upon you.

               Now and for evermore.

ALL: AMEN.

Closing song   **Shout for joy**

1.   Shout for joy! The Lord has let us feast,
        heaven's own fare has fed the last and least;
        Christ's own peace is shared again on earth;
        God the Spirit fills us with new worth.

2.   No more doubting, no more senseless dread:
        God's good self has graced our wine and bread;
        all the wonder heaven has kept in store
        now is ours to keep for evermore.

3.   Celebrate with saints who dine on high,
        witnesses that love can never die.
        Hallelujah! thus their voices ring:
        nothing less in gratitude we bring.

4.   Praise the Maker, praise the Maker's Son,
        praise the Spirit three yet ever one;
        praise the God whose food and friends avow
        heaven starts here! The Kingdom beckons now.

Or: **Sisters and brothers with one voice**

1.   Sisters and brothers, with one voice
        confirm your calling and rejoice:
        each is God's child and each God's choice.
        Alleluia! Alleluia! Alleluia!

2.   Strangers no more, but cherished friends
     live as the body God intends,
     sharing the light the Spirit lends.
     Alleluia! Alleluia! Alleluia!

3.   Not, though, by wisdom, wealth or skill,
     nor by ourselves can we fulfil
     what, for the world, is God's own will.
     Alleluia! Alleluia! Alleluia!

4.   Christ is the way. By him alone
     seeds of the kingdom's life are sown
     patterns of heaven on earth are shown.
     Alleluia! Alleluia! Alleluia!

5.   Then follow him through every day.
     Fear not what crowds or critics say:
     Those on the move stir those who stay.
     Alleluia! Alleluia! Alleluia!

6.   In factory, office, home or hall
     where people struggle, strive or stall,
     seek out and serve the Lord of all.
     Alleluia! Alleluia! Alleluia!

7.   Seeking and serving with one voice,
     confirm your calling and rejoice:
     each is God's child and each God's choice.
     Alleluia! Alleluia! Alleluia!

Or: **We rejoice to be God's chosen**

1.   We rejoice to be God's chosen,
        not through virtue, work or skill,
        but because God's love is generous
        unconformed to human will.
        And because God's love is restless
        like the surging of the sea,
        we are pulled by heaven's dynamic
        to become, not just to be.

2.   We rejoice to be God's chosen,
        to be gathered to God's side
        not to build a pious ghetto
        or be steeped in selfish pride;
        but to celebrate the goodness
        of the One who sets us free
        from the smallness of our vision
        to become, not just to be.

3.   We rejoice to be God's chosen,
        to align with heaven's intent,
        to await where we are summoned,
        and accept where we are sent.
        We rejoice to be God's chosen
        and amidst all that we see,
        to anticipate with wonder
        that the best is yet to be.

Dismissal

Leader: Let us go into the world rejoicing.

It is Christ who goes before us.

ALL: THANKS BE TO GOD. AMEN.

*(Following the service everyone is invited to come for tea in the cloisters.
Also, as you leave the church, you will be handed a small oatcake and be
invited to share it with a stranger. Through this tradition we continue our
celebration together out in the place of the common life.)*

EXTRA RESOURCES FOR THE SUNDAY MORNING COMMUNION

Prayer of Confession and Restoration

(After the call to prayer:)

Leader: Eternal God, maker of the skies above,

lowly Christ, born amidst the growing earth,

Spirit of life, wind over the flowing waters,

in earth, sea and sky,

you are there.

O hidden mystery,

sun behind all suns,

soul behind all souls,

in everything we touch,

in everyone we meet,

your presence is around us,

and we give you thanks.

But when we have not touched

but trampled you in creation,

when we have not met

but missed you in one another,

when we have not received

but rejected you in the poor,

forgive us,

and hear now our plea for mercy.

(The spoken or sung response is followed by these words:)

Leader: Hear now the words of Jesus

for all who are truly sorry

and seek to renew their lives:

Your sins are forgiven.

Go in peace;

come and follow me.

(pause)

Lead us now, O God,

to acknowledge your costly generosity

by living as forgiven people,

until heaven and earth rejoice

and the whole earth cries Glory!

through Christ our Lord.

AMEN.

Prayers of intercession

(The following or another form of prayer may be used. A spoken or sung response may be appropriate.)

Leader: It is in this mystery of communion with Christ

that we pray for the Church throughout the world,

praying in particular for …

We pray for the people and communities of faith

from whom we have come

and to whom we shall return …

We pray for the sick, the bereaved, the oppressed

and the homeless,

praying in particular for …

We pray for the broken and torn fabric of the earth

as it yearns for healing,

praying in particular for …

And because you are one with us, O Christ,

enable us to share your life with the world

by sharing our own lives with the world.

And so we pray, in the words you have taught us:

ALL: OUR FATHER IN HEAVEN …

The Invitation

Celebrant: The table of bread and wine is now to be made ready.

It is the table of company with Jesus,

and all who love him.

It is the table of sharing with the poor of the world,

with whom Jesus identified himself.

It is the table of communion with the earth,

in which Christ became incarnate.

So come to this table,

you who have much faith

and you who would like to have more;

you who have been here often

and you who have not been for a long time;

you who have tried to follow Jesus,

and you who have failed;

Come.

It is Christ who invites us to meet him here.

The Story of the Last Supper

Celebrant: Blessed is our brother Jesus,

who walks with us the road of our world's suffering,

and who is known to us in the breaking of bread.

On the night of his arrest Jesus took bread

and having blessed it

he broke the bread

and gave it to his disciples, saying,

This is my body, given to you.

In the same way he took wine

and having given thanks for it

he poured it out

and gave the cup to his disciples, saying,

This cup is the new relationship with God,

sealed with my blood.

Take this and share it.

I shall drink wine with you next

in the coming Kingdom of God.

(All sit or kneel for prayer)

Celebrant: Let us pray:

ALL: LOVING GOD, THROUGH YOUR GOODNESS ... (see p44)

The prayer of Thanksgiving

Celebrant: The Lord be with you ...

We offer you praise, dear God,

and hearts lifted high,

for in the communion of your love

Christ comes close to us

and we come close to Christ.

Therefore with the whole realm of nature around us,

with earth, sea and sky,

we sing to you.

With the angels of light who envelop us,

with Michael and the host of heaven,

with all the saints before and beside us,

with Columba and Brigid, Patrick and Margaret,

with brothers and sisters, east and west,

we sing to you.

And with our loved ones,

separate from us now,

who yet in this mystery are close to us,

we join in the song of your unending greatness.

(This leads into the Sanctus and Benedictus – see p45)

The prayer of Consecration:

Celebrant: Hear us, O Christ,

and breathe your Spirit upon us

and upon this bread and wine.

May they become for us your body,

vibrant with your life,

healing, renewing and making us whole.

And as the bread and wine which we now eat and drink

are changed into us,

may we be changed again into you,

bone of your bone,

flesh of your flesh,

loving and caring in the world.

The Communion

(The Agnus Dei is followed by:)

Celebrant: Look,

the Body of Christ is broken

for the life of the world.

Here is Christ coming to us in bread and in wine.

The gifts of God

for the people of God.

Sharing of the Peace *(The people are invited to stand)*

Celebrant: Many grains were gathered together to make this bread,

many grapes were mixed to make this wine.

So we who are many,

and come from many places,

are one in Christ.

May the peace of Christ be with you.

ALL: AND ALSO WITH YOU.

Celebrant: Let us greet one another with the sign of peace.

A SERVICE OF WELCOME

Welcome

Opening responses

Leader:	Creator of the world, eternal God,
ALL:	WE HAVE COME FROM MANY PLACES
	FOR A LITTLE WHILE.

Leader:	Redeemer of humanity, God-with-us,
ALL:	WE HAVE COME WITH ALL OUR DIFFERENCES,
	SEEKING COMMON GROUND.

Leader:	Spirit of unity, go-between God,
ALL:	WE HAVE COME ON JOURNEYS OF OUR OWN,
	TO A PLACE WHERE JOURNEYS MEET.

Leader:	So here, in this shelter house,
	let us take time together.
	For when paths cross and pilgrims gather,
	there is much to share and celebrate
ALL:	IN YOUR NAME, THREE-IN-ONE GOD,
	PATTERN OF COMMUNITY. AMEN.

Song

Bible reading *(which may be followed by a brief reflection)*

Sign of welcome *(in which we are invited to greet one another)*

(Sometimes a formal dialogue or rune of hospitality may be used at this point. See extra resources, p61.)

Prayer and the Lord's Prayer

ALL: OUR FATHER IN HEAVEN,

HALLOWED BE YOUR NAME,

YOUR KINGDOM COME,

YOUR WILL BE DONE ON EARTH AS IN HEAVEN,

GIVE US TODAY OUR DAILY BREAD,

FORGIVE US OUR SINS

AS WE FORGIVE THOSE WHO SIN AGAINST US,

SAVE US IN THE TIME OF TRIAL

AND DELIVER US FROM EVIL,

FOR THE KINGDOM, THE POWER

AND THE GLORY ARE YOURS,

NOW AND FOR EVER. AMEN.

Song

Closing prayer

Closing responses and blessing

Leader: The blessing of the Trinity …

ALL: THE BLESSING OF GOD

Leader: who is in this place and every place;

ALL: THE BLESSING OF JESUS

Leader: who is among us, often unrecognised;

ALL:	THE BLESSING OF THE HOLY SPIRIT
Leader:	encouraging us to welcome, and to feel at home;
ALL:	… BE WITH US ALL.
Leader:	As we greet each other, sharing this place and time,
	may our life in community reflect the dance of the Trinity,
	by which the world is blessed.
ALL:	AMEN.

EXTRA RESOURCES FOR THE SERVICE OF WELCOME

Alternative opening responses

Leader: The God of heaven has made a home on earth,

ALL: CHRIST DWELLS AMONG US AND IS ONE WITH US.

Leader: The highest in all creation lives among the least,

ALL: CHRIST JOURNEYS WITH THE REJECTED

AND WELCOMES THE WEARY.

Leader: Come now all who thirst

ALL: AND DRINK THE WATER OF LIFE.

Leader: Come now all who hunger

ALL: AND BE FILLED WITH GOOD THINGS.

Leader: Come now all who seek

ALL: AND BE WARMED BY THE FIRE OF LOVE.

Scripture readings

Words from Jesus concerning welcome, such as Matthew 10:40–42, or stories of welcome and acceptance in Jesus' life and elsewhere in the scriptures, such as Genesis 18:1–14

A sign of welcome

People are encouraged to greet those around them, or someone they do not know. To help facilitate conversation, they could further be asked, for instance, to share their name and why they were given it, or to exchange

with their neighbour a stone, shell or other object received on entering the church. Music may be played to help draw this to a close.

Sometimes, after the sign of welcome, the following dialogue or rune of hospitality may be used:

Optional dialogue

Those already here:	Welcome, you come in God's name.
Those just arrived:	God's blessing on this place, your home.
ALL:	YOU BRING US NEW INSIGHTS AND ENERGY.

Those already here:	You open up to us a wider world.
Those just arrived:	You offer us a space to be ourselves.
ALL:	WE SHARE GOD'S CARE AND CHALLENGE;
	OFFERING AND RECEIVING WELCOME
	WE BECOME CHRIST TO ONE ANOTHER.

Or:

Rune of hospitality

Leader:	Let us stand and say together the words of an old Celtic rune of hospitality:

ALL:	WE SAW A STRANGER YESTERDAY,
	WE PUT FOOD IN THE EATING PLACE,
	DRINK IN THE DRINKING PLACE,
	MUSIC IN THE LISTENING PLACE
	AND, WITH THE SACRED NAME OF THE TRIUNE GOD,
	HE BLESSED US AND OUR HOUSE,
	OUR CATTLE AND OUR DEAR ONES.

Extra Resources

Leader: As the lark says in her song:

                 Often, often, often, goes Christ in the stranger's guise.

Prayer

(A prayer such as the following is said at this point. Beginning by acknowledging that we have come to a place of welcome, we pray for those who are not in a safe place, and those we have left behind, before praying for the week ahead and ending with the Lord's Prayer.)

Leader: O Christ, we bow before you in this shelter-house of prayer once more to give thanks.

                 Together we gather, celebrating your presence in creation around us, in the flowing air, in the fertile earth, and in the swift running tides of Iona.

                 Together we gather, glad of these strong walls which have given refuge to the broken and the poor through the centuries, aware of the countless prayers of joy and of suffering that have been uttered in this place.

                 O Christ, you have inspired the journeying of your people from all over the world to this island of sanctuary and light. Grace us with your continued presence and inspire us to be a people of hospitality.

                 Christ, in your mercy,

ALL: HEAR OUR PRAYER.

Leader: O Jesus, you sat at table with the betrayed and rejected of Palestine. We pray for those today who do not feel welcomed in their daily lives.

Christ, in your mercy,

ALL: HEAR OUR PRAYER.

Leader: O Jesus, you identified with the naked and with those
         who had no place to lay their heads. We pray for the
         thousands of homeless men and women, old and young,
         in our cities.

         Christ, in your mercy,

ALL: HEAR OUR PRAYER.

Leader: O Jesus, you belonged to a refugee family. We pray for
         the millions of displaced people in our world, and for the
         opening of borders to the nationless.

         Christ, in your mercy,

ALL: HEAR OUR PRAYER.

Leader: O Jesus, you cared for your companions and for the
         little ones who surrounded you. We pray for the people
         whom we have left behind in coming to Iona, for those
         for whom God has given us a special care.

         Christ, in your mercy,

ALL: HEAR OUR PRAYER.

Leader: O Jesus, you prayed that we might be one as you and the
         Father are one. We pray that during this week we may
         feel at home with one another and with you in our midst.

         Christ, in your mercy,

ALL: HEAR OUR PRAYER.

Extra Resources

Leader:	And teach us now, O Christ,
	to pray as brothers and sisters …
ALL:	OUR FATHER …

Closing prayer

(This comes after the second song and before the closing responses and/or blessing)

Leader:	Stay with us Lord,
	since the day is far spent and the night is coming;
	kindle our hearts on the way,
	that we may recognise you in the scriptures,
	in the breaking of the bread,
	and in each other.
ALL:	AMEN.

Or:

Leader:	As the poor widow welcomed Elijah,
	let us be open tonight
	to the richness and miracle in meeting.
	As Abraham and Sarah welcomed passing strangers,
	let us entertain the possibility of angels in disguise.
	Let our eyes be opened,
	that we may recognise in our neighbour
	the divine presence of Christ.
ALL:	AMEN

Alternative blessings

(These could be used in place of the closing responses)

Leader:	The blessing of Martha's welcome,
	the blessing of Mary's listening;
	the blessing of action,
	the blessing of reflection
	the blessing of a God
	who is in each of these, and in each one of us,
	be with us all.
ALL:	AMEN.

Or:

Leader:	May the grace of Jesus Christ, the love of God,
	and the communion of the Holy Spirit be with us all,
	this night and always.
ALL:	AMEN.

Songs   *Suggestions for first song in a welcome service:*

The love of God comes close *(see p199–200)*

Come, Host of heaven *(see p35)*

Gather us in ('Here in this place')

All are welcome ('Let us build a house')

Brother, sister, let me serve you

Christ, be our light ('Longing for light')

Dignity and grace ('When I receive the peace of Christ')

Clap your hands all you nations

I rejoiced when I heard them say

Extra Resources

Chants   *Welcome and Evening themes*

Iona Gloria

Jubilate, everybody

Come all you people

Kindle a flame

Night has fallen *(see p200–201)*

For an Evening theme (second song, or after the blessing) see the songs in the General Resources section C, pages 200 to 206.

E
x
t
r
a

R
e
s
o
u
r
c
e
s

SUNDAY EVENING QUIET TIME

Each Sunday evening at 9.00 pm a service of quiet and free prayer takes place for twenty minutes in the Abbey Church.

In order to help create and maintain an atmosphere of peace and quiet it is helpful to arrive a little early.

The first part of the service consists of prayers for some members of the Iona Community who are being prayed for by the whole Community that day. Following this, people are invited to join in a short period of open prayer and intercession.

The second part of the service, lasting about fifteen minutes, is a time of listening to God. We move away from the active side of prayer and worship, and seek to create an atmosphere in which all are able to become receptive to God in silence.

We know from our experience of listening to one another that it is often difficult to give each other our full attention. Distractions, both from outside and within, can prevent us from being fully present to the other. Listening to God is similar. Most of us live very active lives, and our minds and hearts reflect that busyness. It is hard for us to let go of our concerns and anxieties, and simply be present to God. This calls for a kind of abandonment of our immediate cares in order to give space to a deeper listening. Whereas in other services we may focus on God as being above and beyond us, in the quiet time we turn our attention inwards to the God who dwells within each of us. There is no single physical posture that is the right one for such listening. Whether one sits or kneels or needs to shift position, the important thing is to remain alert to the Spirit of God within.

Spending time with God in quiet is not an escape from the troubles of the world, for the God we encounter within is at the heart of the world's life and struggles as well. And in listening to God we may encounter painful truths about ourselves which, if faced, will free us to be more fully of service to God in the world.

The service ends with the saying of the *Nunc Dimittis* – the words that Simeon prayed upon recognising Christ, for whom he had been silently waiting in humility and faith (Luke 2).

Leader: Now, O God, may your servant go in peace

as you promised,

for my eyes have seen the salvation

which you have prepared for all to see,

a light to enlighten the nations

and the glory of your people.

ALL: AMEN.

Those who wish to remain in prayer and quiet after the service ends are welcome to do so.

RESOURCES FOR THE SUNDAY EVENING QUIET TIME

Welcome

Leader: *(words such as:)*

Every Sunday evening we turn from our more active forms of prayer and worship, and seek to become receptive to God in silence. This time of listening lasts for about fifteen minutes, and ends with the words of the *Nunc Dimittis,* a prayer from the New Testament. After this, if you wish to remain in prayer and quiet as others leave, you are welcome to do so.

But first, before our silence begins, you are invited to join in a short period of open prayer and intercession, starting with those members of the Iona Community who are being prayed for by the whole Community today.

Let us pray:

Prayers

- **A brief introductory prayer**

- **Prayers for the Iona Community Family Group of the day** *ending with:*

Leader: God, in your mercy:
ALL: HEAR OUR PRAYER.

- ***Open or silent prayer***

  (not longer than four minutes)

Reflection

(a very short prayer, reading or poem)

SILENCE

(This lasts for fifteen minutes, ending with:)

The Nunc Dimittis

CONCERNING THE SERVICE OF PRAYER FOR JUSTICE AND PEACE

Every Monday evening, worship in the Abbey Church focuses on our part in the injustices of the world. This is an opportunity to pray for concerns which reflect the commitment of the Iona Community to justice and peace (see below). Prayer and politics belong together, as do confession and commitment to action. This service is based on the belief that God's guidance, judgement and mercy can change situations and people. It is said that people come to Iona looking for peace and quiet and go away looking for peace and justice.

Justice and Peace Commitment

We believe:

- that the Gospel commands us to seek peace founded on justice and that costly reconciliation is at the heart of the Gospel.
- that work for justice, peace and an equitable society is a matter of extreme urgency.
- that God has given us partnership as stewards of creation and that we have a responsibility to live in a right relationship with the whole of God's creation.
- that, handled with integrity, creation can provide for the needs of all, but not for the greed which leads to injustice and inequality, and endangers life on earth.
- that everyone should have the quality and dignity of a full life that requires adequate physical, social and political opportunity, without the oppression of poverty, injustice and fear.
- that social and political action leading to justice for all people and encouraged by prayer and discussion, is a vital work of the Church at all levels.
- that the use or threatened use of nuclear and other weapons of

mass destruction is theologically and morally indefensible and that opposition to their existence is an imperative of the Christian faith.

As Members and Family Groups we will:

- engage in forms of political witness and action, prayerfully and thoughtfully, to promote just and peaceful social, political and economic structures.
- work for a British policy of renunciation of all weapons of mass destruction and for the encouragement of other nations, individually and collectively, to do the same.
- work for the establishment of the United Nations Organisation as the principal organ of international reconciliation and security, in place of military alliances.
- support and promote research and education into non-violent ways of achieving justice, peace and a sustainable global society.
- work for reconciliation within and among nations by international sharing and exchange of experience and people, with particular concern for politically and economically oppressed nations.

A SERVICE OF PRAYER FOR JUSTICE AND PEACE

GATHERING

Welcome

Opening responses

Leader:	O God, who called all life into being,
ALL:	THE EARTH, SEA AND SKY ARE YOURS.

Leader:	Your presence is all around us,
ALL:	EVERY ATOM IS FULL OF YOUR ENERGY.

Leader:	Your Spirit enlivens all who walk the earth,
ALL:	WITH HER WE YEARN FOR JUSTICE TO BE DONE,
Leader	For creation to be freed from bondage,
ALL:	FOR THE HUNGRY TO BE FED,
Leader:	For captives to be released,
ALL:	FOR YOUR KINGDOM OF PEACE TO COME ON EARTH.

Song

WORD

Scripture reading *with a particular justice and peace focus. This may be highlighted by other expressions of the Word, such as other readings, newspaper reports, drama, poetry, testimonies, comment and chants.*

RESPONSE

Prayer of confession

(Song or chant)

The response ...

... may continue with a symbolic action in which the people are invited to join, to declare their engagement with the concern; such as lighting candles, placing stones, ringing a bell, planting seeds or writing ... with a period of silence ... and/or an affirmation of faith, such as one of the following:

Affirmation of faith

Leader: In the midst of hunger and war

ALL: WE CELEBRATE THE PROMISE OF PLENTY AND PEACE.

Leader: In the midst of oppression and tyranny

ALL: WE CELEBRATE THE PROMISE OF SERVICE AND FREEDOM.

Leader: In the midst of doubt and despair

ALL: WE CELEBRATE THE PROMISE OF FAITH AND HOPE.

Leader: In the midst of fear and betrayal

ALL: WE CELEBRATE THE PROMISE OF JOY AND LOYALTY.

Leader: In the midst of hatred and death

ALL: WE CELEBRATE THE PROMISE OF LOVE AND LIFE.

Leader: In the midst of sin and decay

ALL: WE CELEBRATE THE PROMISE OF SALVATION
AND RENEWAL.

Leader: In the midst of death on every side

ALL: WE CELEBRATE THE PROMISE OF THE LIVING CHRIST.

AMEN.

Or:

ALL: WE BELIEVE IN GOD

WHOSE LOVE IS THE SOURCE OF ALL LIFE

AND THE DESIRE OF OUR LIVES,

WHOSE LOVE WAS GIVEN A HUMAN FACE

IN JESUS OF NAZARETH,

WHOSE LOVE WAS CRUCIFIED BY THE EVIL

THAT WAITS TO ENSLAVE US ALL

AND WHOSE LOVE, DEFEATING EVEN DEATH,

IS OUR GLORIOUS PROMISE OF FREEDOM.

THEREFORE, THOUGH WE ARE SOMETIMES FEARFUL

AND FULL OF DOUBT,

IN GOD WE TRUST;

AND, IN THE NAME OF JESUS CHRIST,

WE COMMIT OURSELVES, IN THE SERVICE OF OTHERS,

TO SEEK JUSTICE AND TO LIVE IN PEACE,

TO CARE FOR THE EARTH

AND TO SHARE THE COMMONWEALTH

OF GOD'S GOODNESS,

TO LIVE IN THE FREEDOM OF FORGIVENESS

AND THE POWER OF THE SPIRIT OF LOVE,

AND IN THE COMPANY OF THE FAITHFUL

SO TO BE THE CHURCH,

FOR THE GLORY OF GOD. AMEN.

Prayers of concern and/or celebration

SENDING

Song

Closing responses

Leader: A blessing on you who are poor,

ALL: YOURS IS THE KINGDOM OF GOD.

Leader: A blessing on you who mourn,

ALL: YOU SHALL BE COMFORTED.

Leader: A blessing on you who hunger for justice,

ALL: YOU SHALL BE SATISFIED.

Leader: A blessing on you who make peace,

ALL: YOU SHALL BE CALLED CHILDREN OF GOD.

Leader: A blessing on you who are persecuted
for the cause of right,

ALL: YOURS IS THE KINGDOM OF HEAVEN.
AMEN.

Or: **(alternative response)**

Leader: God, lead us, that we may stand firm in faith for justice.

ALL: TEACH US LOVE. TEACH US COMPASSION.
ABOVE ALL, OUT OF LOVE AND COMPASSION,
TEACH US TO ACT.
AMEN.

Blessing

(which may be followed by a final chant as the people leave)

EXTRA RESOURCES FOR THE SERVICE OF PRAYER FOR JUSTICE AND PEACE

Alternative opening reponses

Leader: Your love is as high as the heavens, O God;
your faithfulness soars through the skies.

ALL: YOUR RIGHTEOUSNESS REACHES THE TOWERING PEAKS;
YOUR JUSTICE THE DEPTHS OF THE SEA.

Leader: We shelter beneath your wings;
we feast on the food you provide.

ALL: WE OPEN OUR EYES TO DRINK IN YOUR GOODNESS;
FOR YOU ARE THE SOURCE OF ALL LIFE,
AND BECAUSE OF YOUR LIGHT WE SEE LIGHT.

Or:

Leader: Creator Spirit, wellspring of our lives,
as the refreshing rain falls on the just and unjust alike

ALL: REFRESH US WITH YOUR MERCY,
WHO KNOWS OUR OWN INJUSTICE.

Leader: As the stream flows steadily on,
defying all the odds of stone and water

ALL: FLOW OVER EVERY BOUNDARY AND BORDER
THAT SEPARATES US FROM EACH OTHER.

Leader: As the waters of our baptism washed us and welcomed us

ALL: RENEW US NOW IN NEWNESS OF LIFE
AND UNITY OF LOVE.

Extra Resources

Leader: As we were once held
           in the waters of our mother's womb
ALL: HOLD US IN THE POWER AND PEACE
           OF YOUR ABIDING PRESENCE.

Chants

Freedom is coming (South Africa)

Senzenina ('What have we done'; South Africa)

Stand firm (Cameroons)

Dona nobis pacem in terra ('Give us peace on earth')

Through our lives and by our prayers

Kindle a flame

Kyrie eleison (Ukraine or Ghana)

Our burden is heavy

Goodness is stronger than evil

Over my head

If you believe and I believe

Give us light, give us light

Songs

Sent by the Lord am I (Nicaragua)

The Lord is my light (former Czechoslovakia)

Jesus Christ is waiting

O Lord my God

Inspired by love and anger

From each one condemned by birth

O Lord hold my hand

The Spirit is moving in my heart

Do not retreat

Charity? ('Do not offer me your money … ')

Heiwa song ('See the children born of sorrow …')

The love burning deep

Liberator Lord ('To those whose lives are bitter …')

Song for love ('Now we sing to praise love's blessing …')

Gather us in

Make me a channel of your peace

Don't tell me of a faith that fears

We will not take what is not ours

How can we stand together

Poor folk won't always be forgotten

Come now O Prince of Peace

Heaven shall not wait

Till all the jails are empty

Touch the earth lightly

Oh the earth is the Lord's

For the fruits of all creation

When our Lord walked the earth (see p206)

There is a line of women (see p207)

To be a soldier (see p209)

Old Testament:	Gen 9:8–17; Deut 30:6–8,11–15; 1 Sam 2:1–10;
	Ps 9; 10; 51; 72:1–15; 96; 97; 98; 113; 140:1–8,12–13;
	Isa 2:1–5; 55:6–13; 58:1–12; 61:1–4; 63:15–17;
	Jer 31:31–34; Hosea 11:1–10; Micah 4:1–4; 6:1–3,6–8;
	Amos 5:7,10–24; Malachi 3:1–5.

Extra Resources

New Testament: Mt 5:1–12; 16:24–26; 28:1–10; Mk 1:14–15; Lk 4:16–30;
6:20–36; 12:13–21,32–34; 18:18–29; Jn 20:19–22;
20:24–29; Acts 4:32–36; 1 Pet 3:8–17; James 2:1–5;
5:1–6; Eph 2:13–22; Gal 6:1–5; 2 Cor 8:1–9.

Prayers of confession

1.　　O God, you are always true to us in love
　　　and we are left wanting to say sorry
　　　for our faithlessness to you and to one another,
　　　for our forgetting of the poor and the broken,
　　　for our failure to cherish creation.
　　　Give us life, O God, to change
　　　and enable us to change, that we may live.

2.　　O God, gladly we live and move and have our being in you.
　　　Yet always in the midst of this creation-glory,
　　　we see sin's shadow and feel death's darkness:
　　　around us in the earth, sea and sky, the abuse of matter;
　　　beside us in the broken, the hungry and the poor,
　　　the betrayal of one another;
　　　and often, deep within us, a striving against your Spirit.
　　　O Trinity of love,
　　　forgive us that we may forgive one another,
　　　heal us that we may be people of healing,
　　　and renew us that we also may be makers of peace.

Alternative affirmations

A Christian Aid affirmation

(This may be read responsively by two groups)

A: We believe that God hopes and works for a world
where all shall be included in the feast of life,
and that in Christ we see how costly it is
to bring that world about.

B: We believe that God's strategy for a new world
is to put the poorest first,
and that nothing is more important for God's people
than to bring the poor good news.

A: We believe that rich and poor alike
can be generous, wise and creative
because all are made in God's image,
and that all are made poorer when they are left out.

B: We confess that we use our strength to protect ourselves
and order the world to benefit the rich and not the poor,
and that none of us can be trusted with too much power
over others.

A: We believe that loving our neighbours
means working for justice,
so that all have a say in what happens to them.

B: We believe that God made the good earth
to sustain and delight us,
and that we are called to take care of it and enjoy it.

Extra Resources

Extra Resources

A: We believe that the God of all the earth is at work
beyond the churches as well as within them,
making common cause with all who want the poor
to be included.

B: We long for the time
when the meek shall inherit the earth
and all who hunger and thirst after justice
shall be satisfied,
and we believe that, despite the persistence of evil,
now is always the time
when more good can be done
and we can make a difference.

*(This affirmation was created to accompany Christian Aid's
Statement of Faith, and is included here by permission.)*

Or: • Affirmation from South Africa

Leader: It is not true that this world and its inhabitants are
doomed to die and be lost;

ALL: THIS IS TRUE: FOR GOD SO LOVED THE WORLD THAT HE
GAVE HIS ONLY SON SO THAT EVERYONE WHO BELIEVES
IN HIM SHALL NOT DIE, BUT HAVE EVERLASTING LIFE.

Leader: It is not true that we must accept inhumanity and
discrimination, hunger and poverty,
death and destruction;

ALL: THIS IS TRUE: I HAVE COME THAT THEY MAY HAVE LIFE,
AND HAVE IT ABUNDANTLY.

Leader: It is not true that violence and hatred shall have the last

word, and that war and destruction have come to stay
for ever;

ALL: THIS IS TRUE: FOR TO US A CHILD IS BORN, TO US A SON
IS GIVEN, IN WHOM AUTHORITY WILL REST, AND WHOSE
NAME WILL BE PRINCE OF PEACE.

Leader: It is not true that we are simply victims of the powers of
evil that seek to rule the world;

ALL: THIS IS TRUE: TO ME IS GIVEN AUTHORITY IN HEAVEN
AND ON EARTH, AND LO, I AM WITH YOU ALWAYS, TO THE
END OF THE WORLD.

Leader: It is not true that we have to wait for those who are
specially gifted, who are the prophets of the church,
before we can do anything;

ALL: THIS IS TRUE: I WILL POUR OUT MY SPIRIT ON ALL
PEOPLE, AND YOUR SONS AND DAUGHTERS SHALL
PROPHESY, YOUR YOUNG PEOPLE SHALL SEE VISIONS,
AND YOUR OLD FOLK SHALL DREAM DREAMS.

Leader: It is not true that our dreams of liberation of humankind,
our dreams of justice, of human dignity, of peace, are not
meant for this earth and its history;

ALL: THIS IS TRUE: THE HOUR COMES, AND IT IS NOW, THAT
TRUE WORSHIPPERS SHALL WORSHIP GOD IN SPIRIT
AND IN TRUTH.

Or: **Magnificat affirmation**

Leader: Let us celebrate and affirm our faith in the word's of
Mary's song:

E
x
t
r
a

R
e
s
o
u
r
c
e
s

My heart praises you, O God,

ALL: MY SPIRIT REJOICES IN YOU, MY SAVIOUR.

Leader: You have remembered me in my lowliness,

ALL: AND NOW I WILL BE CALLED BLESSED.

Leader: You have done great things for me

ALL: AND SHOWN MERCY TO ALL THOSE WHO TRUST YOU.

Leader: You have stretched out your right arm

ALL: AND SCATTERED THE PROUD WITH ALL THEIR PLANS.

Leader: You have brought down the mighty from their thrones

ALL: AND LIFTED UP THE LOWLY.

Leader: You have filled the hungry with good things

ALL: AND SENT THE RICH AWAY WITH EMPTY HANDS.

Leader: You have kept your promise to our mothers and fathers,

ALL: AND COME TO THE HELP OF YOUR PEOPLE,

            TO ABRAHAM AND TO SARAH,

            AND TO ALL GENERATIONS FOR EVER. AMEN.

Prayers of concern

1.   O God of all creation

        who has come to us in Jesus,

        lead us in your way of love

        and fill us with your Spirit.

        Choose us

        to bring good news to the poor,

        to proclaim liberty to the captives,

to bring sight to the blind

and set free the oppressed.

So shall your new creation come

and your will be done.

Amen.

2.   Spirit of truth and judgement,

who alone can cast out

the powers that grip our world

at the point of crisis,

give us your discernment,

that we may accurately name what is evil,

and know the way that leads to peace,

through Jesus Christ,

Amen.

3.   Spirit of integrity,

you drive us into the desert

to search out our truth.

Give us clarity to know what is right,

that we may abandon the false innocence

of failing to choose at all,

but may follow the purposes of Jesus Christ.

Amen.

4.   God of history,

you share our joys and crushing sorrows,

you hear the cries of the afflicted,

you fill the hungry,

and you set free the oppressed.

E
x
t
r
a

R
e
s
o
u
r
c
e
s

We pray for the end to all injustice.

Inspire us with the all-embracing love of God,

challenge us with the sacrificial love of Jesus,

empower us with the transforming love of the Spirit,

that we and all God's children may live and be free!

Amen.

Alternative closing responses:

Leader: Christ has come to turn the world upside down:

ALL: TO HUMBLE THE POWERFUL AND TO LIFT UP THE LOWLY.

Leader: Christ has come to turn the tables:

ALL: TO TOPPLE VAIN IDOLS AND TO STAND WITH THE POOR.

Leader: Christ has come to proclaim God's kingdom:

Men: to feed the hungry,

Women: to give sight to the blind,

Men: to strengthen the weary,

Women: to set the prisoners free.

Leader: Christ has come to turn the world upside down:

ALL: TO OVERTHROW THE PRESENT ORDER

WITH A REVOLUTION OF LOVE.

Blessing

May the God who shakes heaven and earth,

whom death could not contain,

who lives to disturb and heal us,

bless you with power to go forth

and proclaim the Gospel.

Amen.

Or:

> May God write a message upon your heart,
>
> bless and direct you,
>
> then send you out
>
> living letters of the Word.
>
> Amen.

For other justice and peace material, see the Extra Resources for General Worship, especially responses Witnesses for peace *and* Blessing the world *in section A, and the Communion blessing* As you have been fed *in section B. Also see material relating to the* Afternoon Prayers for Justice and Peace.

E
x
t
r
a

R
e
s
o
u
r
c
e
s

CONCERNING PRAYERS FOR HEALING AND THE LAYING-ON OF HANDS

This service of prayers for healing, which takes place every Tuesday evening, reflects our belief that God's purpose for us all is a life of wholeness, as expressed in the life and teaching of Jesus. The ministry of healing is an integral part of our Christian witness.

We each stand in need of healing, but in this ministry we recognise also the social dimension. The healing of divided communities and nations, and the healing of the earth itself, have their place alongside the healing of broken bodies, hurt minds and wounded hearts, and of the hurts and divisions within ourselves. So too our prayers are complementary to the work of medicine and other forms of healing, which are also channels of God's loving and transforming purpose.

In our service we shall name particular people, places and situations for which prayers have been specifically asked. We do this because each person and situation is known to God, not as a problem to be solved, but as a focus for God's acceptance and love. We are not seeking to change God but to change the world; and we trust God that our prayers will be answered, although we do not know when or how healing will happen.

There will also be an opportunity for those who wish to come forward to receive or share in the ministry of the laying-on of hands. This can be either for themselves or for another person or situation. In and through this we affirm that the ministry of healing is not restricted to particular individuals but is a corporate, inclusive process – the work of the whole Christian community in which we all have a part to play. God's healing purpose, the promise of God's fulfilling and sustaining love, is for every one of us. Whether we choose to come forward or to remain seated in prayer and concern, God can use our presence in this service.

The Iona Prayer Circle

Iona is the centre of a prayer fellowship of women and men from all over the world committed to praying for people whose names are on our monthly intercessions list. Further information about joining the Prayer Circle, or about having a name added to the monthly list, can be obtained from the Prayer Circle Secretary, via the Abbey Office.

A SERVICE OF PRAYER FOR HEALING

Welcome

Opening responses

Leader: We gather here in your presence, God,

ALL: IN OUR NEED,
AND BRINGING WITH US THE NEEDS OF THE WORLD.

Leader: We come to you, for you come to us in Jesus,

ALL: AND YOU KNOW BY EXPERIENCE
WHAT HUMAN LIFE IS LIKE.

Leader: We come with our faith and with our doubts;

ALL: WE COME WITH OUR HOPES AND WITH OUR FEARS.

Leader: We come as we are, because you invite us to come;

ALL: AND YOU HAVE PROMISED NEVER TO TURN US AWAY.

Song

Scripture reading

Prayers of intercession

The invitation

Song

(At the end of this song, those who wish to receive the prayer and the laying-on of hands are asked to come and take a place at one of the kneelers set out, and those who wish to share in the ministry should come and stand behind them. If all the places are occupied, please wait until the first group have received the laying-on of hands. They will move back to allow others to take their place.)

Prayer for the laying-on of hands

ALL: SPIRIT OF THE LIVING GOD, PRESENT WITH US NOW,

ENTER YOU, BODY, MIND AND SPIRIT,

AND HEAL YOU OF ALL THAT HARMS YOU,

IN JESUS' NAME. AMEN.

Closing prayer and blessing

EXTRA RESOURCES FOR THE SERVICE OF PRAYER FOR HEALING

Welcome

*(As part of the welcome it is helpful to explain **very briefly** to people the shape of the service as outlined in `Concerning Prayer for Healing' (p88) with particular reference to the opportunity of receiving prayer and the laying-on of hands in the second half of the service.)*

Scripture reading

(Stories of healing from the Gospels, such as Mark 1:29–45, as well as Psalms, such as Psalm 42, and other passages imploring God's aid are help-ful readings to include in the service.)

Songs

We lay our broken world

Stumbling blocks and stepping stones

Thirsting for God

A touching place

Take this moment

We cannot measure how you heal

The Lord is my light

Lord of life, we come to you

Lord, we come to ask your healing

Love is the touch

Mallaig sprinkling song ('Spirit of God, come dwell')

Whoever lives beside the Lord

As a deer longs for running streams

Oh the life of the world

My shepherd is the Lord

O God, you are my God alone

Chants

(to be used as response to the readings or to the prayers of intercession)

Nada te turbe ('Let nothing worry you')

Kyrie eleison ('Lord have mercy')

Jesu Christe miserere ('Jesus Christ have mercy')

Stay with me

O Lord hear my prayer

Bless the Lord my soul

Lord Jesus Christ, lover of all

God to enfold you

Be still and know

I waited, I waited on the Lord

Lord, draw near

Prayers of intercession

Leader: Let us pray, as we now bring before God

those for whom prayer has been requested:

Loving God,

you share with us the care of creation,

and call each of us by name.

We remember that those who encountered Jesus

found acceptance, healing and the possibility of new life;

Extra Resources

that the disciples, though imperfect human beings,

through prayer and touch helped others to find healing

in the power of your Holy Spirit.

And so, in the name of the Triune God, we pray …

(followed by the lists of intercession. Suggested headings are included at the end of this section.* It is best to have someone else assisting in the prayers of intercession and also in the laying-on of hands.)

The invitation   *(the following words may be used)*

Leader: At the end of the next song if you wish to seek prayer, for yourself, on behalf of someone, or for a crisis in the world, you are invited to come and take it in turn to kneel or stand at one of the cushions.

Also, if you wish to share in the laying-on of hands, please come forward and place a hand on the shoulder or arm of the person in front of or next to you.

Or you may choose to take part by remaining seated in your place and joining in the prayer for the laying-on of hands on page 91.

Jesus says, 'Come to me all you who are troubled and I will give you rest.' So come, you who are burdened by regrets and anxieties, you who are broken in body or in spirit, you who are torn by relationships and by doubt, you who feel deeply within yourselves the divisions and injustices of our world. Come, for Jesus invites us to bring him our brokenness.

Our song is …

Prayer before the laying-on of hands

> God, our Creator, we are held in your everlasting arms.
>
> Jesus, our Saviour, we are healed by your wounded hands.
>
> Holy Spirit, be present as we reach out to one another in love.

Or: Living God, breathe your Spirit upon us

> and surround us with your love.
>
> Giving Jesus, grant us your compassion.
>
> Healing Spirit, come and bring us peace.

(and then proceed to the prayer for the laying-on of hands)

Closing prayer and blessing

> Watch now, dear Lord,
>
> with those who wake or watch or weep tonight,
>
> and give your angels charge over those who sleep.
>
> Tend your sick ones, O Lord Christ,
>
> rest your weary ones,
>
> bless your dying ones, soothe your suffering ones,
>
> pity your afflicted ones, shield your joyous ones,
>
> and all for your love's sake.
>
> Amen.

> And now may the God of hope
>
> fill us with all joy and peace in believing,
>
> that we may abound in hope
>
> in the power of the Holy Spirit.
>
> Amen.

Extra Resources

*Suggested headings for prayers of intercession

(A sung response may sometimes be used between some or all the groups of intercessions.)

Loving God, we hold in your healing presence those who suffer pain and ill-health, with their families, friends and those who care for them: …
… May they know the deep peace of Christ.

Loving God, we hold in your healing presence those who suffer in mind and spirit, and all who care for them: …
… May they know the deep peace of Christ.

Loving God, we hold in your healing presence the suffering people of our world, and the places where people are experiencing division, injustice and violence: …
… May they know the deep peace of Christ.

Loving God, we hold in your healing presence those struggling to overcome addiction or abuse, those supporting and working with them, and all whose suffering has distanced them from those who love: …
… May they know the deep peace of Christ.

Loving God, we hold in your healing presence those facing bereavement. We also pray for those who have died: …
… May they know the deep peace of Christ.

Loving God, we give you thanks for health restored and prayers answered: …
We hold in your healing presence and peace those whose

needs are not known to us: …

And those whose names we do not know, but who are known
to you, and for whom we have been asked to pray.

And we name in our hearts those who are close to us.

… May they know the deep peace of Christ.

May your wisdom, God, guide nurses, doctors and those who
work in every part of our Health Service and across the world.
We pray also for those who work in the coastguard, rescue and
emergency services.

(The intercessions conclude with the following prayer or another:)

God of compassion and love,

we offer you all our suffering and pain.

Give us strength to bear our weakness,

healing even when there is no cure,

peace in the midst of turmoil

and love to fill the spaces in our lives.

Glory to God, from whom all love flows,

glory to Jesus, who showed his love through suffering,

and glory to the Holy Spirit,

who brings light to the darkest places.

Amen.

CONCERNING THE ACT OF COMMITMENT SERVICE

`Will you come and follow me?' These are the words of Jesus that give shape to our Wednesday evening liturgy. It is a simple service of personal commitment to Jesus in response to his love. For some it will be a commitment for the first time, while for others it will be a re-commitment to the One whom they have been following as the Way, the Truth and the Life.

St Augustine warned Christians of the fourth century not to de-capitate the risen Christ – that is, not to separate Jesus from the rest of his Body on earth, and therefore not to pretend that we can love Jesus while neglecting to love our brothers and sisters. On a Wednesday evening the call for commitment to Jesus is at the same time a call for commitment to all that Jesus identifies himself with. We are not to separate what God has joined together, and so an act of commitment to Jesus is at the same time an act of commitment to the brothers and sisters throughout the world who journey with Jesus (1 John 4), just as it is a commitment to the suffering and the poor of the world with whom Jesus inseparably identified himself (Matt. 25), and to caring for the earth, sea and sky which God called into being through the Word (John 1).

By Wednesday evening many in the Abbey Church will be think-ing about the situations to which they will soon return. The act of commitment can be a way of confirming the new perspectives or heal-ings or convictions that we have received on Iona, and thus help to prepare the path for integrating the Iona experience with our day to day situations.

During the service there is opportunity to make an outward sign of commitment through some form of symbolic action and by affirming our faith. At the same time we receive the blessing of God and promise of Jesus.

While the call to commitment is for each one of us, we respond in different ways and at different times. People should not feel under any obligation to move forward, or that not doing so is reflective of their level of commitment. Many choose to remain at prayer in their places to renew a commitment to Jesus. Everyone is encouraged to participate in the service in the way that is most helpful to them.

AN ACT OF COMMITMENT SERVICE

Welcome

Opening responses

Leader:	Jesus says, 'I am the Way for you.'
ALL:	AND SO WE COME TO FOLLOW CHRIST.

Leader:	Jesus says, 'I am the Truth for you.'
ALL:	AND SO WE COME TO DWELL IN THE LIGHT.

Leader:	Jesus says, 'I am the Life for you.'
ALL:	AND SO WE COME,
	LEAVING BEHIND ALL ELSE TO WHICH WE CLING.

Song

Scripture

Invitation to commitment

Song

Sign of commitment and promise

Prayer
and/or affirmation and commitment *(such as the following:)*

Leader:	We are not alone;
	we live in God's world.

ALL: WE BELIEVE IN GOD:

WHO HAS CREATED AND IS CREATING,

WHO HAS COME IN JESUS,

THE WORD MADE FLESH,

TO RECONCILE AND MAKE NEW,

WHO WORKS IN US AND OTHERS

BY THE SPIRIT.

WE TRUST IN GOD.

WE ARE CALLED TO BE THE CHURCH:

TO CELEBRATE GOD'S PRESENCE,

TO LIVE WITH RESPECT IN CREATION,

TO LOVE AND SERVE OTHERS,

TO SEEK JUSTICE AND RESIST EVIL,

TO PROCLAIM JESUS, CRUCIFIED AND RISEN,

OUR JUDGE AND OUR HOPE.

IN LIFE, IN DEATH, IN LIFE BEYOND DEATH,

GOD IS WITH US.

WE ARE NOT ALONE.

THANKS BE TO GOD. AMEN.

Song

Closing responses

Leader: Look at your hands, see the touch and the tenderness,

ALL: GOD'S OWN FOR THE WORLD.

Leader: Look at your feet, see the path and the direction,

ALL: GOD'S OWN FOR THE WORLD.

Leader:	Look at your heart, see the fire and the love,
ALL:	GOD'S OWN FOR THE WORLD.
Leader:	Look at the cross, see God's Son and our Saviour,
ALL:	GOD'S OWN FOR THE WORLD.
Leader:	This is God's world,
ALL:	AND WE WILL SERVE GOD IN IT.

Promise and blessing

Leader:	Jesus said, 'I am with you always.'
	May God the Creator bless you.
	May God the Son walk with you.
	May God the Spirit lead your lives with love.
ALL:	AMEN.

(As you leave the church there is opportunity to make an offering towards the work of the Iona Community.)

EXTRA RESOURCES FOR THE SERVICE OF COMMITMENT

Welcome

*(As part of the welcome it is helpful to explain **very briefly** to the congregation the shape of the service as outlined in Concerning the Act of Commitment Service' (p98), with particular reference to the opportunity to make a sign of commitment in the service.)*

Scripture reading

(Stories from Jesus' life in which he calls people to follow him, such as Matthew 19:16–30, are helpful readings for this service.)

Reflection

(A brief expansion of the scripture reading, along the theme of commitment, may follow the reading or may be incorporated into the invitation to commitment.)

Songs

Come take my hand

The summons ('Will you come and follow me')

Sing hey for the carpenter

Lord Jesus Christ

Jesus Christ is waiting

The Spirit is moving in my heart

Take this moment, sign and space

Oh, where are you going

I am the vine

Extra Resources

Brother, sister, let me serve you

When our confidence in God is shaken

Chants

(to be used as response to the readings or at other points in the service)

Through our lives and by our prayers

Yesuve saranam ('Jesus I surrender')

Jesu tawa pano ('Jesus, we are here for you')

Thuma mina ('Send me Jesus')

Sent by the Lord am I

Invitation to commitment

(The Leader explains that there will be an opportunity for an outward sign of commitment – a way of making a promise to God or ourselves, of marking this moment in our journey. The Leader describes the form this action will take, and makes clear that it is equally acceptable not to participate but to take the time for silent reflection instead. The following words of invitation can then be used.)

> So come and follow Jesus,
> you who have committed yourselves already,
> and you who would like to do so for the first time;
> you who have given yourselves to the care of creation
> and to the suffering ones of the world,
> and you who feel moved by the Spirit
> to begin to offer yourselves;
> you who have been faithful in your life commitments
> and you who have failed.

Extra Resources

Come, for our Lord invites us to follow him,

and to make new beginnings in our lives.

Sign of commitment and blessing

A variety of symbolic actions are possible – lighting candles, pinning notes to a cross, placing a stone in water, etc. Sometimes different points in the church can be used for different actions, e.g. lighting a candle in the South Aisle Chapel, as a sign of waiting before God; receiving a drop of water on the hand or forehead at the Font, to renew a baptismal promise; writing on a paper in the North Transept, to make a commitment to act.

In this service any action should have an element of receiving as well as giving. People could be asked to take their lighted candle back to their seat, or could be anointed with oil, be given a stone, or receive a piece of paper with one of the words of Jesus. A blessing, such as the one below, may be said at the end of the action.

In the traditional form of the service, people are invited to come up to the Communion Table and kneel in rows, so that those leading the service can place a hand on the shoulder of each in turn, saying words of Jesus (see below).

Prayer

Before the action begins, a brief prayer such as the following may be said:

O God of the high heavens,

O Christ of the deep earth,

O Spirit of the flowing waters,

O Trinity of love,

you have offered your love to us,

and here we pledge our love to you.

Strengthen us in our desire,

and breathe into our bodies the passion of your love.

We pray this in the name of Jesus,

to whom we commit ourselves.

Amen.

The words of Jesus

(It is best to have a second person assisting in the action and the words)

Hear now the words of Jesus spoken to each one of us.

Jesus says:

My peace I give to you.

Do not be afraid.

I call you my friend.

Abide in my love.

Even the hairs of your head are numbered.

Follow me.

I am the way for you.

I am the life for you.

I am the truth for you.

Blessed are your eyes for they see.

You are my witness.

You are my brother.

I am hungry, give me food.

I am in prison, come to me.

I am thirsty, give me drink.

I am a stranger, welcome me.

I am naked, clothe me.

I am sick, visit me.

Abide in me and I in you.

I will drink wine with you in the Kingdom of God.

You will shine like the sun.

You are in me and I in you.

Ask and it will be given you.

Seek and you will find.

Knock and the door will be opened to you.

I am the vine, you are the branch.

I will give you rest.

You are the light of the world.

You are the salt of the earth.

You are my sister.

Give and it will be given to you.

Love others as I have loved you.

The truth will make you free.

Feed my sheep.

Watch and pray.

I am with you always.

(Many other words of Jesus can appropriately be included, but it is advisable to keep as simple phrases as possible and to maintain direct speech in the sayings.)

Alternative affirmations and commitments

*(An affirmation, such as the one in the main order, or one of these below,
could be used after the action or, when the words of Jesus are used, at an
earlier point in the service.)*

Leader:	Let us affirm our faith.
ALL:	WE BELIEVE IN JESUS CHRIST,
	SON OF THE ONE GOD,
	MAKER AND SUSTAINER OF EARTH, SEA AND SKY.
	BORN OF MARY'S WOMB,
	FAITHFUL TO THE GOD OF ABRAHAM AND SARAH,
	JESUS HEALED THE SICK,
	SERVED THE POOR,
	AND PROCLAIMED HEAVEN ON EARTH.
	CONDEMNED BY THE RELIGIOUS,
	CRUCIFIED BY THE STATE,
	HE DIED
	BUT TRANSFORMED EVEN DEATH
	AND ROSE TO LIFE EVERLASTING.
	HE BLESSED THE DISCIPLES WITH HIS HOLY SPIRIT
	AND SENT THEM FORTH,
	EAST AND WEST, NORTH AND SOUTH.
	WE COMMIT OURSELVES
	TO JESUS,
	TO ONE ANOTHER AS BROTHERS AND SISTERS
	AND TO HIS MISSION IN THE WORLD
	IN THE GRACE OF THE HOLY SPIRIT.
	AMEN.

Extra Resources

Or:

Leader: Let us affirm our faith

ALL: WE BELIEVE THAT GOD IS PRESENT

IN THE DARKNESS BEFORE DAWN;

IN THE WAITING AND UNCERTAINTY

WHERE FEAR AND COURAGE JOIN HANDS,

CONFLICT AND CARING LINK ARMS,

AND THE SUN RISES OVER BARBED WIRE.

WE BELIEVE IN A WITH-US GOD

WHO SITS DOWN IN OUR MIDST

TO SHARE OUR HUMANITY.

WE AFFIRM A FAITH

THAT TAKES US BEYOND THE SAFE PLACE:

INTO ACTION, INTO VULNERABILITY

AND INTO THE STREETS.

WE COMMIT OURSELVES TO WORK FOR CHANGE

AND PUT OURSELVES ON THE LINE;

TO BEAR RESPONSIBILITY, TAKE RISKS,

LIVE POWERFULLY AND FACE HUMILIATION;

TO STAND WITH THOSE ON THE EDGE;

TO CHOOSE LIFE

AND BE USED BY THE SPIRIT

FOR GOD'S NEW COMMUNITY OF HOPE.

AMEN.

Or:

blazing

L: WE BELIEVE IN A BRIGHT AND AMAZING GOD,

WHO HAS BEEN TO THE DEPTHS OF DESPAIR

ON OUR BEHALF;

P: WHO HAS RISEN IN SPLENDOUR AND MAJESTY;

L: WHO DECORATES THE UNIVERSE

WITH SPARKLING WATER, CLEAR WHITE LIGHT,

P: TWINKLING STARS AND SHARP COLOURS,

OVER AND OVER AGAIN.

L: WE BELIEVE THAT JESUS IS THE LIGHT OF THE WORLD;

THAT GOD BELIEVES IN US, AND TRUSTS US,

P: EVEN THOUGH WE MAKE THE SAME MISTAKES

OVER AND OVER AGAIN.

L: WE COMMIT OURSELVES

TO JESUS,

P: TO ONE ANOTHER AS BROTHERS AND SISTERS,

AND TO THE MAKER'S BUSINESS IN THE WORLD.

L: GOD SAID: LET THERE BE LIGHT.

P: AMEN. *and that light shines in the darkness.*

AN EVENING SERVICE OF COMMUNION

Welcome and invitation

Opening responses

Leader: We light a light in the name of the Maker,
who lit the world and breathed the breath of life for us …

We light a light in the name of the Son,
who saved the world and stretched out his hand to us …

We light a light in the name of the Spirit,
who encompasses the world
and blesses our souls with yearning …

ALL: WE LIGHT THREE LIGHTS FOR THE TRINITY OF LOVE:
GOD ABOVE US, GOD BESIDE US, GOD BENEATH US:
THE BEGINNING, THE END, THE EVERLASTING ONE.

Prayer of invocation

Song

The Word   *(Scripture reading and brief reflection)*

Communion song or chant

Story of the Last Supper

Prayer of Thanksgiving

The Blessing of the bread and wine

Prayers of concern

(during which there may be opportunity to offer free prayer in one's own language, or to speak names into the silence)

... ending with **The Lord's Prayer**

The Breaking and Sharing of the bread and wine

(As we share communion, we serve one another by passing the bread and the wine around the table)

A sign of peace

(We offer each other a sign of peace)

Chant or song

Closing responses

Leader:	On our hearts and on our houses,
ALL:	THE BLESSING OF GOD.
Leader:	In our coming and our going,
ALL:	THE PEACE OF GOD.
Leader:	In our life and our believing,
ALL:	THE LOVE OF GOD.
Leader:	At our end and new beginning,
ALL:	THE ARMS OF GOD TO WELCOME US AND BRING US HOME.
	AMEN.

EXTRA RESOURCES FOR AN EVENING SERVICE OF COMMUNION

Welcome

(This includes words of invitation to people of all ages and traditions)

Prayer of invocation

> Come, Lord Jesus, be our guest,
>
> stay with us for day is ending.
>
> With friend, with stranger,
>
> with young and with old,
>
> be among us tonight.
>
> Come close to us that we may come close to you.
>
> Forgive us that we may forgive one another.
>
> Renew us so that, where we have failed,
>
> we may begin again. Amen.

The Story of the Last Supper

> Among friends, gathered round a table,
>
> Jesus took bread,
>
> and, having blessed it,
>
> he broke the bread
>
> and gave it to his disciples, saying,
>
> 'This is my body which is given for you.'
>
> In the same way he took wine,
>
> and, having given thanks for it,
>
> he poured it out

Extra Resources

and gave the cup to his disciples, saying,

'This cup is the new relationship with God,

sealed with my blood.

Take this and share it.

I shall drink wine with you next

in the coming kingdom of God.'

So now, following Jesus' example,

we take this bread and this wine;

the ordinary things of the world

through which God will bless us.

And, as Jesus offered thanks for the gifts of the earth,

let us also celebrate God's goodness.

The prayer of Thanksgiving

Blessed are you, O God,

for you have brought forth bread from the earth.

Blessed are you, O God,

for you have created the fruit of the vine.

In the beginning you watered the earth

that man and woman might have food and drink.

You gave to your servant Sarah

bread to strengthen her family on their journey,

and wine to make them glad.

You called Moses and his people out of bondage

and refreshed them with food in the wilderness.

You gave Mary and Jesus their daily bread to share.

And here at your table

you offer us bread and wine for the journey

to nourish us as sons and daughters.

And so with all our sisters and brothers,

before us and beside us,

we praise you from our hearts for your unending greatness.

The Blessing of the bread and the wine

Lord Jesus Christ,

present with us now,

as we do in this place what you did in an upstairs room,

breathe your Spirit upon us

and upon this bread and this wine,

that they may be heaven's food and drink for us,

renewing, sustaining and making us whole,

and that we may be your body on earth,

loving and caring in the world.

The prayers of concern

(The following prayer can be used to introduce a brief time of free prayer or silence; or a more informal invitation to offer prayer, or to call out names of people and places, can be given. The prayers of concern are concluded with the Lord's Prayer, which the people may be invited to say in their own traditions or languages.)

You are above us, O God,

You are beneath.

You are in air, you are in earth,

you are beside us, you are within.

O God, you are in the betrayed and suffering people

of our world

just as you were in the broken body of Jesus.

We pray now for all that concerns us

as we sit at table together.

Let us offer our own prayers

Both spoken and unspoken.

The Breaking and Sharing of the bread and wine

Look,

the Bread of Heaven is broken for the life of the world.

The gifts of God for the people of God.

A sign of peace

Leader: The peace of Christ is here to stay!

Let us share his peace with one another.

Songs

The song of the supper

God's table

The Lord of all

Love is the welcome

These I lay down

O give thanks to the Lord

Bread is blessed and broken

One bread, one body

Put peace into each other's hands

I will always bless the Lord *(p197–8)*

Chants

We come to share our story

Holy, holy (various)

We sing your glory

Kyrie eleison (various)

Jesu Christe miserere

Eat this bread

Thuma mina

Recessional chants

Alleluia (various)

We are marching

Amen alleluia

Amen siakudumisa

Sanna

Extra Resources

AN ALTERNATIVE COMMUNION LITURGY

The drama of Creation

Leader:	In the beginning, God made the world:
<u>*Women*</u>:	Made it and mothered it,
<u>*Men*</u>:	Shaped it and fathered it;
<u>*Women*</u>:	Filled it with seed and with signs of fertility,
<u>*Men*</u>:	Filled it with life and with song and variety.
Leader:	All that is green, blue, deep and growing,
ALL:	GOD'S IS THE HAND THAT CREATED YOU.
Leader:	All that is tender, firm, fragrant and curious,
ALL:	GOD'S IS THE HAND THAT CREATED YOU.
Leader:	All that crawls, flies, swims, walks or is motionless,
ALL:	GOD'S IS THE HAND THAT CREATED YOU.
Leader:	All that speaks, sings, cries, laughs or keeps silence,
ALL:	GOD'S IS THE HAND THAT CREATED YOU.
Leader:	All that suffers, lacks, limps or longs for an end,
ALL:	GOD'S IS THE HAND THAT CREATED YOU.
Leader:	The world belongs to God,
ALL:	THE EARTH AND ALL ITS PEOPLE.

Prayer of invocation

Song

The drama of Incarnation

Leader:	When the time was right, God sent the Son.
<u>*Women*</u>*:*	Sent him and suckled him,
<u>*Men*</u>*:*	Reared him and risked him;
<u>*Women*</u>*:*	Filled him with laughter and tears and compassion,
<u>*Men*</u>*:*	Filled him with anger and love and devotion.
Leader:	Unwelcomed child, refugee and runaway,
ALL:	CHRIST IS GOD'S OWN SON.
Leader:	Skilled carpenter and homeless wayfarer,
ALL:	CHRIST IS GOD'S OWN SON.
Leader:	Feeder and teacher, healer and antagonist,
ALL:	CHRIST IS GOD'S OWN SON.
Leader:	Lover of the unlovable, toucher of the untouchable, forgiver of the unforgivable,
ALL:	CHRIST IS GOD'S OWN SON.
Leader:	Loved by the least, feared by the leaders; befriended by the weak, despised by the strong; deserted by his listeners, denied by his friends; bone of our bone, flesh of our flesh, writing heaven's pardon over earth's mistakes,
ALL:	CHRIST IS GOD'S OWN SON.
Leader:	The Word became flesh,
ALL:	HE LIVED AMONG US, HE WAS ONE OF US.

The Word

(Scripture readings, reflections, drama, movement, etc.)

The drama of Salvation

Leader:	When the world could wait no longer,
Women:	The carpenters took up their tools,
Men:	They made a cross for God's own son,
Women:	Fashioned from wood and skill of human hands,
Men:	Fashioned from hate and will of human minds.
Leader:	He was a man of sorrows and acquainted with grief,
ALL:	FOR US HE GRIEVED.

Leader:	He was summoned to the judgement hall,
	an enemy of the state, a danger to religion,
ALL:	BY US HE WAS JUDGED.

Leader:	He was lashed with tongues and scourged with thongs,
ALL:	BY HIS STRIPES WE ARE HEALED.

Leader:	He was nailed to the cross by human hands,
ALL:	BONE OF OUR BONE, FLESH OF OUR FLESH.

Leader:	He died, declaring God's forgiveness.
	He rose on the third day, transforming death.
	He ascended into heaven,
	that he might be everywhere on earth.
	He sent the Holy Spirit as the seal of his intention.
	He sets before us bread and wine,
	and invites us to his table.
	This is the place where we are made well again.
ALL:	AND ALL WILL BE MADE WELL.

Leader:	For God sent the Son into the world

not to condemn the world,

ALL: BUT THAT THE WORLD THROUGH HIM MIGHT BE SAVED.

Invitation

Song

The Story of the Last Supper

Prayer of Thanksgiving *(ending with 'Holy Holy')*

The Blessing of the bread and wine

The prayers of intercession

(during which there is opportunity to offer prayer in one's own language, followed by the people's sung response)

The Breaking and Sharing of the bread and wine

(during which we serve one another around the table with the bread and wine)

Sharing a sign of peace

The drama of celebration

Leader: In the end as in the beginning, God is God:

Women: Loved by us, wanted by us,

Men: Praised by us, served by us;

Women: Filling the folk with the gifts of the Spirit,

Men:	Making them whole for the good of the earth.
Leader:	For bread and wine, this place and this time,
ALL:	THANKS BE TO GOD.
Leader:	For the peace we are promised
	which the world won't destroy,
ALL:	THANKS BE TO GOD.
Leader:	For the hope of heaven on earth
	and the final song of joy,
ALL:	THANKS BE TO GOD.

Blessing

Chant   *(or song)*

CONCERNING THE AGAPE

The Agape is a fellowship meal, a very ancient tradition of the Church. In the Abbey we sit round a long table for this service – the same table that we use when we share Communion together on a Thursday evening. Here it is always an open table: the invitation to share Communion is offered to everyone. There are still those, however, who feel excluded by a sacrament about which Christians can have such different under-standings. Sometimes an Agape may be the more appropriate way of expressing our unity in Christ.

The Agape, using oatcakes, water or, according to the occasion, something else special, is sacramental in the sense that every shared meal, and every aspect of our life as God's children, on God's good earth, can be called sacramental. It is a service that can be led by lay people. So it is also a celebration of the ministry of the whole people of God. That's you and me.

In this service we celebrate our life together in community.

AN AGAPE

Welcome

Opening responses

Leader:	Out of darkness came light;
ALL:	AND THE POWER OF GOD WAS REVEALED
Men:	in the running wave and the flowing air,
Women:	in the quiet earth and the shining stars.

Leader:	Out of the dust came life;
ALL:	AND THE IMAGE OF GOD WAS REVEALED
Men:	in the human face and the gentle heart,
Women:	in the warmth of flesh and the depth of soul.

Leader:	Out of justice came freedom;
ALL:	AND THE WISDOM OF GOD WAS REVEALED
Men:	in the need to grow and the will to love,
Women:	in the chance to know and the power to choose.

Leader:	And God looked at the creation,
ALL:	AND BEHOLD, IT WAS VERY GOOD.

Song

Prayers of adoration

Reader:	I will keep on thanking God
	with constant words of prayer.
	I will glory in the living God:
	the humble will hear and be glad.

(This is followed by the prayer of adoration)

Prayer of confession

Reader: Salt is good, but if salt has lost its saltiness, how can you season it?

Leader: Giving God, you blessed us with saltiness,
ALL: BUT WE BECAME BLAND.

Leader: You trusted us with your Word,
ALL: BUT WE DID NOT KEEP IT.

Leader: You lit a flame in our midst,
ALL: BUT WE HID IT UNDER FORMALITY,
SMOTHERED IT WITH OUR FEARS.

Leader: God, in your mercy:
ALL: FORGIVE US.

(silence)

Leader: Forgiving God, we believe that you have called us
ALL: TO BE SALT AND LIGHT;
Leader: that you offer us time and space and strength
ALL: TO BEGIN AGAIN.

(silence)

Leader: Giving and forgiving God,
ALL: WE THANK YOU.

Reader: Have salt in yourself, and be at peace with one another.

A sign of peace

(We share the peace of Christ with each other.)

Giving thanks for the week

The Word   *(Scripture reading and brief reflection)*

Introduction to the Sharing

Reader: Taste and see that God is good.

Sharing

Prayer   … ending with **The Lord's Prayer**

Song

Closing responses

Leader: O God of life, of all life and of each life,
we lay our lives before you;
we give our lives to you
from whom nothing in us is hidden.

Women: You are before us, God, you are behind.
Men: You are around us, God, you are within.

Leader: O God of life, O generous Spirit,
ALL: RENEW US WITH YOUR LIFE,
TONIGHT, TOMORROW AND ALWAYS.

Blessing

EXTRA RESOURCES FOR THE AGAPE

Prayer of adoration

Reader: … the humble will hear and be glad.

(Here the following prayer can be used:)

Leader   Let us pray.

Living God, our loving parent: you cherish your creation
and we praise you.
With earth, air, water, fire: in our element as your children,
we praise you.
With our lips, with our lives,
in all our diversity, each one made in your image,
we praise you.
Because, in Jesus, you came to share
our human lives, our sorrow and joy,
we praise you.
Because your Spirit is at work today:
encouraging, enabling, surprising us,
we praise you.
Poor as we are, you give us hope:
salt of the earth, you give us meaning and purpose
and we praise you.

ALL: AMEN.

Extra Resources

Giving thanks for the week

People are invited to call out single words or brief phrases. A simple response may be used, such as, Generous God: WE THANK YOU.

Or a short chant may be used instead of any spoken words, such as:

> Glory and gratitude and praise
> now let earth to heaven raise.
> Glory and gratitude and praise
> these we offer to God.

Introduction to the Sharing

<u>*Reader:*</u>   Taste and see that God is good.

(Here the Leader gives simple instructions to make sure all are included in the sharing)

The Sharing

Oatcakes with honey, sweet Christmas bread, or charoseth (grated apples formed into balls with chopped nuts, raisins, honey and cinnamon) are examples of food that could be shared, with water, squash or mulled wine to drink (poured into tumblers from jugs on the table and passed around).

Prayer   *(at the conclusion of the Sharing)*

Leader: As we share these oatcakes,
          as we taste this honey,
          as we pour out this water,

we thank you, God, for our daily bread

for the food which delights and nourishes us

and for companionship that sustains us.

We thank you, too, for clean, cool water

to quench our thirst,

and for the Living Water

with which you surprise and enrich

and transform our lives.

ALL: AMEN.

(followed by the Lord's Prayer, in our own languages and traditions)

Blessing

Leader: God bless each of us as we travel on.

In our times of need

may we find a table spread in the wilderness

and companions on the road.

ALL: AMEN.

Or:

Leader: Giving God,

bless all who have gathered round this table.

May we know the fullness of your presence

at every meal and in all our sharing.

ALL: AMEN.

(This may be followed by a recessional chant)

Bible quotations: Before and after the confession: Mark 9:50

Before the prayer of adoration: Psalm 34:1

In the introduction to the sharing: Psalm 34:8

Songs

God's table ('Since the world was young')

For the fruits of all creation

I will always bless the Lord *(see p197–8)*

Welcome to the feast *(see opposite)*

(Also some of the songs and chants listed in the Extra Resources for Evening Communion)

Welcome to the feast

(Can be sung to *Bleanwern*, *Hyfrodol* or *Abbot's Leigh*)

1. Light the candles, bring your presents,
   let us celebrate good days,
   with rejoicing and thanksgiving,
   for great actions give God praise.
   Now's the time for jubilation,
   lift your voice in joyful song;
   thanks for justice, Christ-like anger,
   friendships made through righting wrong.

2. In the shining of the candles
   dust shows up as in the sun
   thus revealing all our failings,
   power misused and work not done.
   In our praying: God forgive us,
   Let's remember those reviled:
   folk exploited, women wordless,
   children who have never smiled.

3. Light the candle in the darkness,
   flames will penetrate the night;
   pass the brightness to your neighbours
   till the world is full of light.
   Act with justice, use your anger,
   be on God's side, choose the least;
   God, in weakness, will receive us,
   calling us to share their feast.

Extra Resources

CREATION LITURGY

Opening responses

Leader: Let the light fall warm and red on the rock,

let the birds sing their evening song

and let God's people say Amen.

ALL: AMEN.

Leader: Let the tools be stored away,

let the work be over and done

and let God's people say Amen.

ALL: AMEN.

Leader: Let the flowers close and the stars appear,

let hearts be glad and minds be calm

and let God's people say Amen.

ALL: AMEN.

Song

Psalm or reading *(concerning creation)*

Confession

Leader: O God,

your fertile earth is slowly being stripped of its riches,

ALL: OPEN OUR EYES TO SEE.

Leader: O God,

your living waters are slowly being choked with chemicals,

ALL: OPEN OUR EYES TO SEE.

Leader: O God,

your clear air is slowly being filled with pollutants,

ALL: OPEN OUR EYES TO SEE.

Leader: O God,

your creatures are slowly dying

and your people are suffering,

ALL: OPEN OUR EYES TO SEE.

Leader: God our maker, so move us by the wonder of creation,

ALL: THAT WE REPENT AND CARE MORE DEEPLY.

Leader: So move us to grieve the loss of life,

ALL: THAT WE LEARN TO CHERISH AND PROTECT YOUR WORLD.

Chant

(during which there will be an action in which we commit ourselves to caring for God's earth or we celebrate the goodness of God's earth)

Prayer of gratitude and concern

Song

Closing responses

Leader: This we know, the earth does not belong to us,

ALL: WE BELONG TO THE EARTH.

Leader: This we know, all things are connected,

ALL: LIKE THE BLOOD THAT UNITES ONE FAMILY.

Leader:	This we know, we did not weave the web of life,
ALL:	WE ARE MERELY A STRAND IN IT.

Leader:	This we know, whatever we do to the web,
ALL:	WE DO TO OURSELVES.

Leader:	Let us give thanks for the gift of creation,
ALL:	LET US GIVE THANKS THAT ALL THINGS HOLD TOGETHER IN CHRIST.

Blessing

Leader:	Bless to us, O God,
	the moon that is above us,
	the earth that is beneath us,
	the friends who are around us,
	your image deep within us,
ALL:	AMEN.

EXTRA RESOURCES FOR THE CREATION LITURGY

Opening responses *(alternative)*

Leader: Let the darkness of night surround us,

let light and warmth gather us

and let God's people say Amen.

ALL: AMEN.

Leader: Let the tools be stored away,

let the work be over and done

and let God's people say Amen.

ALL: AMEN.

Leader: Let the winds blow wild around us,

but let hearts be glad and minds be calm

and let God's people say Amen.

ALL: AMEN.

Songs

Many and great (Native Indian tradition)

You are author and Lord of creation (Nepal)

The song is love ('What is the song …')

Sing praise to God

Blessing and honour

From creation's start

I am for you ('Before the world began')

Lord your hands (Philippines)

Sing out, earth and skies

Oh the life of the world

Abundant life ('We cannot own the sunlit sky')

For the fruits of all creation

For your generous providing

Touch the earth lightly

The peace of the earth be with you

Dance and sing

Readings (scriptures)

Psalms 19:1–6; 23:1–6; 29:1–11; 46:2–11; 65:6–14; 67:1–7; 72:1–19; 80:2–20; 84:2–13; 85:2–14; 89:2–17; 96:1–13; 97:1–12; 100:1–5; 104:1–35; 131:1–3; 147:1–11; 148:1–14.

Wisdom 7:22–30. Job 38 & 39 Ecclesiasticus 42:15–26; 43:1–28.

Colossians 1:15–20; 3:11. Ephesians 1:17–23. Romans 8:18–25.

Readings from the mystics

A. *From: Meditations with Hildegard of Bingen*

> The earth is at the same time mother.
>
> She is mother of all that is natural,
>
> mother of all that is human.
>
> She is mother of all,
>
> for contained in her are the seeds of all.
>
> The earth of humankind contains all moistness,
>
> all verdancy,
>
> all germinating power.

It is in so many ways fruitful.

All creation comes from it,
yet it forms not only the basic raw material for humankind
but also the substance of the incarnation of God's Son.

B. *From:*　*Meditations with Julian of Norwich*

I saw that God was everything that is good
and encouraging.

God is our clothing
that wraps, clasps and encloses us
so as never to leave us.

God showed me in my palm
a little thing round as a ball
about the size of a hazelnut.

I looked at it with the eye of my understanding
and asked myself:
'What is this thing?'
And I was answered: 'It is everything that is created.'

I wondered how it could survive since it seemed so little
it could suddenly disintegrate into nothing.

The answer came: 'It endures and ever will endure,
because God loves it.'

And so everything has being because of God's love.

C. *From: Meditations with Meister Eckhart*

> Apprehend God in all things,
>
> for God is in all things.
>
> Every single creature is full of God
>
> and is a book about God.
>
> Every creature is a word of God.
>
> If I spent enough time with the tiniest creature –
>
> even a caterpillar –
>
> I would never have to prepare a sermon.
>
> So full of God
>
> is every creature.

Prayers of concern

Prayer of intercession based on Colossians 1:15–20

O Christ, your cross speaks both to us and to our world.

In your dying for us
you accepted the pain and hurt of the whole of creation.

The arms of your cross stretch out
across the broken world in reconciliation.

You have made peace with us.
Help us to make peace with you
by sharing in your reconciling work.

May we recognise your spirit

disturbing and challenging us to care for creation
and for the poor who most feel the effects of its abuse.

O Christ, the whole of creation groans.
Set us free and make us whole.

Prayer of intercession based on Ephesians 4:7–16

There is no pain in our hearts or in our planet
that you do not know,
for you have touched the lowest places on earth.

Teach us to grieve with you, O Christ,
the loss of all the beauty that is being killed.

There is no place in the heavens
that cannot be touched by your resurrection presence,
for you fill all things.

Give us strength in your victory over death
to grow into your way of love,
which does not despair but keeps sowing seeds of hope
and making signs of wholeness.

Under Christ's control
all the different parts of the body fit together
and the whole body is held together
by every joint with which it is provided.

Teach us to know our interconnectedness with all things.
Teach us to grow with each other
and all living creatures through love.

Extra Resources

E
x
t
r
a

R
e
s
o
u
r
c
e
s

Actions

Some actions may be better placed after the prayers of intercession as with the following examples:

- *People to light candles around a cross to signify their share in reconciling creation to God (Colossians 1:15–20).*
- *People to add stones to a spiral of growth at the foot of a cross committing themselves to growing in God's way of love for creation and grieving the crucifixion of life on earth (Ephesians 4:7–16).*

Chants

Kindle a flame

Dona nobis pacem in terra ('Give us peace on earth')

Kyrie eleison ('Lord have mercy': Ghana)

Mayenziwe ('Your will be done': South Africa)

Your kingdom come O Lord (Russia)

Agios o theos ('Holy God have mercy': Russia)

Come Holy Spirit

A SIMPLE EVENING LITURGY

Opening responses

Leader: Peace on each one who comes in need,

ALL: PEACE ON EACH ONE WHO COMES IN JOY.

Leader: Peace on each one who offers prayers,

ALL: PEACE ON EACH ONE WHO OFFERS SONG.

Leader: Peace of the Maker, Peace of the Son,

ALL: PEACE OF THE SPIRIT, THE TRIUNE ONE.

Song

Prayer

Leader: O God, for your love for us, warm and brooding,

which has brought us to birth and opened our eyes

to the wonder and beauty of creation,

ALL: WE GIVE YOU THANKS.

Leader: For your love for us, wild and freeing,

which has awakened us to the energy of creation:

to the sap that flows,

the blood that pulses,

the heart that sings.

ALL: WE GIVE YOU THANKS.

Leader: For your love for us, compassionate and patient,

which has carried us through our pain,

wept beside us in our sin,

and waited with us in our confusion.

ALL: WE GIVE YOU THANKS.

Leader: For your love for us, strong and challenging,

which has called us to risk for you,

asked for the best in us,

and shown us how to serve.

ALL: WE GIVE YOU THANKS.

Leader: O God we come to celebrate

that your Holy Spirit is present deep within us,

and at the heart of all life.

Forgive us when we forget your gift of love

made known to us in Jesus,

and draw us into your presence.

The Word of God

Song

Sharing of the day

(The leader invites the company to share a brief word or picture from today which is special in some way.)

Prayer

(Here is opportunity for prayers of concern, spoken or unspoken, each prayer being followed by a chant.)

We bring to God

someone whom we have met or remembered today

and for whom we want to pray

(Chant)

We bring to God

someone who is hurting tonight and needs our prayer

(Chant)

We bring to God

a troubled situation in our world tonight

(Chant)

We bring to God, silently,

someone whom we find hard to forgive or trust

(Chant)

We bring ourselves to God

that we might grow in generosity of spirit,

clarity of mind,

and warmth of affection.

(Chant)

Song

Closing responses

Leader: O Trinity of Love,

You have been with us at the world's beginning,

ALL: BE WITH US TILL THE WORLD'S END.

Leader: You have been with us at our life's shaping,

ALL: BE WITH US AT OUR LIFE'S END.

Leader: You have been with us at the sun's rising,

ALL: BE WITH US TILL THE DAY'S END.

             AMEN.

Blessing

A CELTIC EVENING LITURGY

Opening responses

Leader: Come to us this night, O God,

ALL: COME TO US WITH LIGHT.

             (Here a candle may be lit and placed centrally)

Leader: Speak to us this night, O God,

ALL: SPEAK TO US YOUR TRUTH.

             (Here a Bible may be placed centrally)

Leader: Dwell with us this night, O God,

ALL: DWELL WITH US IN LOVE.

             (Here a cross may be placed centrally)

Song

Prayer of thanksgiving

Leader: Thanks be to you O Christ,

ALL: FOR THE MANY GIFTS YOU HAVE BESTOWED ON US,

             EACH DAY AND NIGHT, EACH SEA AND LAND,

             EACH WEATHER FAIR, EACH CALM, EACH WILD.

Leader: Each night may we remember your mercy

             given so gently and generously.

ALL: EACH THING WE HAVE RECEIVED,

             FROM YOU IT CAME;

             EACH THING FOR WHICH WE HOPE,

             FROM YOUR LOVE IT WILL COME;

             EACH THING WE ENJOY,

IT IS OF YOUR BOUNTY;

EACH THING WE ASK,

COMES OF YOUR DISPOSING.

Leader: O God, from whom each thing that is, freely flows,

ALL: GRANT THAT NO TIE OVER STRICT, NO TIE OVER DEAR,

MAY BE BETWEEN OURSELVES AND THIS WORLD.

AMEN.

The word of God

Leader: O God, as these words are read,

ALL: IN OUR HEARTS MAY WE FEEL YOUR PRESENCE.

Reader: (a portion of scripture)

Song

Affirmation of faith

ALL: WE BELIEVE, O GOD OF ALL GODS,

THAT YOU ARE THE ETERNAL GOD OF LIFE,

WE BELIEVE, O GOD OF ALL GODS,

THAT YOU ARE THE ETERNAL GOD OF LOVE.

Men: We believe, O God and Maker of all creation,

that you are the creator of the high heavens,

that you are the creator of the deep seas,

that you are the creator of the stable earth.

Women: We believe, O God of all the peoples,

that you created our souls and set their warp,

that you created our bodies and gave them breath,

that you made us in your own image.

ALL: WE GIVE YOU OUR WORSHIP

WITH OUR WHOLE LIVES,

WE GIVE YOU OUR ASSENT

WITH OUR WHOLE POWER,

WE GIVE YOU OUR EXISTENCE

WITH OUR WHOLE MIND,

WE GIVE YOU OUR KNEELING

WITH OUR WHOLE DESIRE.

Prayers of concern

Leader: O Christ, kindle in our hearts within

a flame of love to our neighbour,

to our foes, to our friends, to our kindred all.

ALL: O CHRIST OF THE POOR AND THE YEARNING,

FROM THE HUMBLEST THING THAT LIVES

TO THE NAME THAT IS HIGHEST OF ALL,

KINDLE IN OUR HEARTS WITHIN

A FLAME OF LOVE.

(Here a ring of votive candles may be lit around the symbols, followed by a period of silence)

Or:

(Each person may have a candle which will be lit from neighbour to neighbour, followed by a period of intercessions, freely spoken or unspoken)

(At the end of this time the following prayer will be said:)

Leader: We are placing our souls and our bodies

under your guarding this night, O Christ.

ALL: O SON OF THE TEARS, OF THE WOUNDS, OF THE PIERCINGS,

MAY YOUR CROSS THIS NIGHT BE SHIELDING ALL.

Song

Blessing

Leader: Be the great God between your shoulders

to protect you in your going and your coming;

be the Son of Mary near your heart;

and be the perfect Spirit upon you pouring.

ALL: AMEN.

AFTERNOON PRAYERS FOR JUSTICE AND PEACE

Welcome

Opening responses

Leader: Creator of the cosmos,
             of eternity and time:
ALL: BE WITH US IN *THIS* TIME.

Leader: Saviour of the world,
             healer of the nations:
ALL: BE WITH US IN THIS PLACE.

Leader: Breath of all that lives,
             of people near and far:
ALL: STIR WITHIN OUR LIVES.

Leader: Maker-Spirit-Son,
             God of here and now:
ALL: BE PRESENT IN OUR WORSHIP,
             THAT WE MAY FIND NEW WAYS
             TO BE PRESENT IN YOUR WORLD.

Or:

Leader: In the peace and the bustle of island life:
             the sounds of creation.
ALL: RUNNING WAVE AND RESTLESS EARTH,
             FLOWING AIR AND SPINNING STARS
             DECLARE THE SON OF PEACE.

(silence)

Leader: In the activity and stillness of an ancient church:

the cries of a broken world.

ALL: ANGRY AND HOPEFUL CRIES,

HUNGRY UNENDING CRIES

PROCLAIM THE CROSS OF CHRIST.

(silence)

Leader: In the silence and turmoil of our hearts:

the voice of the Risen One.

ALL: COMFORT TO THE SUFFERER,

CHALLENGE TO THE FOLLOWER,

THE CALL OF CHRIST TO ALL.

(silence)

Or:

Leader: We are called from the ends of the earth,

ALL: WE ARE CALLED FROM THE CENTRE OF OUR LIVES.

Leader: Men and women, young and old,

ALL: RICH AND POOR, STRONG AND WEAK.

Leader: We are called into God's love,

ALL: TO YEARN FOR JUSTICE AND TO PRAY FOR PEACE.

Introductory prayer

Bible reading

Reflection

Song

Concluding prayers and blessing:

A: ***Working for justice and peace***

ALL: O GOD, LEAD US FROM DEATH TO LIFE,

FROM FALSEHOOD TO TRUTH.

LEAD US FROM DESPAIR TO HOPE,

FROM FEAR TO TRUST.

LEAD US FROM HATE TO LOVE,

FROM WAR TO PEACE.

LET PEACE FILL OUR HEARTS,

OUR WORLD, OUR UNIVERSE. AMEN.

(The Universal Prayer for Peace)

Leader: Peace to the nations, east and west,

peace to our neighbours, black and white,

peace to all women, peace to all men,

the peace of Christ above all peace.

ALL: AMEN.

B: ***Building community***

ALL: O GOD,

SINCE THERE IS NO DISTINCTION OF RACE AND ORIGIN,

IN YOU WE ARE ALL ONE.

EMPOWER US TO BREAK DOWN

THE BARRIERS THAT STILL DIVIDE US,

SO THAT WE MAY WORK IN HARMONY

WITH EACH OTHER AND WITH YOU

(The Council of Churches for Britain and Ireland)

Leader: May God bless you and keep you,

            may God's face shine on you and give you grace,

            may God's eyes light upon you and bring you peace.

ALL: AMEN.

C: *Creating a just economic order*

ALL: MAKE US WORTHY, O LORD, TO SERVE

            THE MEN AND WOMEN THROUGHOUT THE WORLD

            WHO LIVE AND DIE IN POVERTY AND HUNGER.

            GIVE THEM, THROUGH OUR HANDS,

            THIS DAY THEIR DAILY BREAD,

            AND BY OUR UNDERSTANDING AND LOVE,

            GIVE PEACE AND JOY. AMEN.

                                    (Mother Teresa)

Leader: And may the God of peace give you peace

            at all times and in all ways.

ALL: AMEN.

D: *Dreaming dreams and seeing visions*

ALL: CHRIST, YOU ARE BEFORE US.

            THIS IS WHAT GIVES US COURAGE TO GO ON.

            IT IS YOU WHO DIRECTS.

            IT IS YOU WHO BECKONS.

            SO WE DEDICATE OURSELVES.

            AND WE BLESS YOU NOW.

                                    (George MacLeod)

Leader: And now may the peace of God,

which passes all understanding,

guard your hearts and your thoughts, in Christ Jesus.

ALL: AMEN.

E: ***Honouring creation***

ALL: O CHRIST, THERE IS NO PLANT IN THE GROUND

BUT IT IS FULL OF YOUR VIRTUE.

THERE IS NO FORM IN THE STRAND

BUT IT IS FULL OF YOUR BLESSING.

THERE IS NO LIFE IN THE SEA,

THERE IS NO CREATURE IN THE OCEAN,

THERE IS NOTHING IN THE HEAVENS

BUT PROCLAIMS YOUR GOODNESS.

THERE IS NO BIRD ON THE WING,

THERE IS NO STAR IN THE SKY,

THERE IS NOTHING BENEATH THE SUN

BUT PROCLAIMS YOUR GOODNESS. AMEN.

(A Celtic prayer)

Leader: Deep peace of the running wave to you,

deep peace of the flowing air to you,

deep peace of the quiet earth to you,

deep peace of the shining stars to you,

deep peace of the Son of Peace to you.

ALL: AMEN.

F: *Taking action for justice and peace*

ALL: LORD, MAKE US INSTRUMENTS OF YOUR PEACE.

WHERE THERE IS HATRED, LET US SOW LOVE,

WHERE THERE IS INJURY, PARDON,

WHERE THERE IS DOUBT, FAITH,

WHERE THERE IS DESPAIR, HOPE,

WHERE THERE IS SADNESS, JOY.

O DIVINE MASTER,

GRANT THAT WE MAY NOT SO MUCH SEEK

TO BE CONSOLED AS TO CONSOLE,

TO BE UNDERSTOOD AS TO UNDERSTAND,

TO BE LOVED AS TO LOVE.

FOR IT IS IN GIVING THAT WE RECEIVE,

IT IS IN PARDONING THAT WE ARE PARDONED,

IT IS IN DYING THAT WE ARE BORN AGAIN

TO EVERLASTING LIFE. AMEN.

(St Francis)

Leader: And now may the God of hope bring you

such joy and peace in believing

that you overflow with hope

in the power of the Holy Spirit.

ALL: AMEN.

EXTRA RESOURCES FOR AFTERNOON PRAYERS FOR JUSTICE AND PEACE

The six broad sections A–F allow for a different aspect on each of the six days (Monday to Saturday). The sequence may vary from week to week. Introductory and concluding prayers are also marked A–F to link with the section for the day. There are several themes and suggested Bible passages in each section; and these should be used as a resource, to which worship leaders may wish to add.

Welcome

(during which the leader announces the theme of the service – see below)

Introductory prayers

(The leader follows the opening responses with the prayer for the section A to F from which the theme has been chosen – or another appropriate prayer:)

> **A.**   Loving God,
> you have led us to this place,
> not to shield us from heartache
> and the pain of human life,
> but to heal us and inspire us,
> to gently redirect us,
> till we see the world as you do
> and love it with your love.
> AMEN.

E
x
t
r
a

R
e
s
o
u
r
c
e
s

B.   Forgiving God,

your Son once said

that his brother, sister, mother

were all who did your will.

Yet even when we *fail* to do your will

you welcome and accept us

as your children.

Teach us to include others

as readily as you include us;

for to do so is to do your heavenly will.

AMEN.

C.   Eternal God,

out of your great generosity

you brought the world into being

and gave it life.

Then you gave it yourself,

on the cross of human suffering.

Such priceless, painful giving!

Did you invite us here to show us that?

Then show it to us once more, O God!

Show us a different kind of world,

a different cost of living,

where the pain will not be eased

by the money we spend on ourselves,

but by the way we spend ourselves for others,

and the way we value life.

Eternal God,

out of your great generosity,

make *us* generous; bring *us* into being.

AMEN.

D. Liberator Christ,

you came into a holy place

and read the sacred word

about sight for blind folk and freedom for prisoners.

Come to this place now.

Read these words to *us*

till our own eyes are opened, our faith is unlocked,

and we can see the world as it is,

and as it could be;

till the yearnings of ordinary people are taken seriously,

and the visions of the young are valued,

and the potential of the old is released;

till your kingdom is celebrated everywhere,

and your church is good news to the poor.

AMEN.

E. Here, O Creator God,

we look in wonder at all you have made.

But remind us:

the earth does not belong to us;

we belong to the earth.

And remind us:

the earth, and all that is in it,

belongs to you.

You confront us with such beauty, and such power.

And such responsibility.
Teach us, O Creator God,
to respect this planet, our home,
to live carefully within the web of life,
and to give you the glory.
AMEN.

F.   God in the midst, come close to us,
and help us come close to you,
as, for a fraction of time,
we step back from the activities of the day.
May we treasure such moments with you.
Moments when we can bring to you
the things we are doing,
and find new meaning for them,
and new strength for doing them.
And moments for recalling
how we are meeting you already,
in the stuff of daily living and engagement,
when faith is tested
and compassion is translated into action.
So if, as the day goes on, we forget you,
do not forget us, O God.
AMEN.

Bible reading and reflection

Suggested themes and readings are listed below. The reflection that follows the Bible reading is optional, must be very brief, and can be a relevant comment, poem, newspaper extract, etc.

A: *Working for justice and peace*

A theme connected with any of the following: the peace movement, human rights, oppressive political regimes and those who are oppressed, the use of violence and of torture, racial or sexual or social discrimination.

Non-violence:	Philippians 4:4–7 *or* Romans 12:14–21 *or* John 18:3–12 *or* Isaiah 53:4–7
Refugees and asylum seekers:	Matthew 2:13–15
Unfair trial/torture:	John 19:1–10
Prisoners of conscience:	Acts 12:6–10
Overcoming racism:	Colossians 3:9–15 *or* Luke 10:29–37
Recognition of women:	Luke 24:1–12 *or* Matthew 26:1–13
Rights of children/ the young:	Luke 18:15–17 *or* Matthew 18:1–6
A just society:	Jeremiah 6:13–16 *or* Micah 4:3–4 Psalm 122 *or* Matthew 23:1–4, 23–24, 37

B: *Building community*

A theme connected with any of the following: the health of society, bridge builders, minorities, freedom of speech, prisoners of conscience, broken families and communities, community development workers, church unity, the United Nations.

Extra Resources

Inclusive society:	James 2:1–4, 8–9 *or* Luke 14:15–24
The whole community:	Jonah 3:1–5, 3:10–4:4, 4:11
God is for all:	Acts 10:34–36 *or* Matthew 22:1–10
Freedom of speech/ expression:	Luke 19:35–40
The courage to say no:	Luke 23:13–18, 22–24 *or* John 8:2–11 *or* Daniel 3:13–18 *or* 2 Samuel 12:1–7a
Church unity:	John 17:18–23 *or* 1 Corinthians 12:12–16, 26–27

C: *Creating a just economic order*

A theme connected with any of the following: workers and management in industry, those who are unemployed or whose labour is exploited, poverty and homelessness, equal opportunities.

Wealth and sustainability:	Luke 12:13–21 *or* Luke 12:32–34 *or* Luke 21:1–4
Employment:	Matthew 20:1–16
Just working conditions:	Jeremiah 22:13–17
Exploitation of workers:	John 2:13–16 *or* Amos 8:4–6 *or* James 5:1–6
Poverty/homelessness:	Job 24:1–8 *or* Psalm 113:2–8 *or* Matthew 25:37–40 *or* Luke 2:1–7
International debt:	Leviticus 25:10–14

D: *Dreaming dreams and seeing visions*

A theme connected with any of the following: prophets and pioneers; artists, writers and musicians; spiritual centres and communities of faith; people who are broken, cynical, despairing.

World peace:	Isaiah 2:1–4 *or* Revelation 22:1–2
Social restoration and harmony:	Isaiah 11:3b–9 *or* Isaiah 55:1–3, 12–13
All things new:	Isaiah 43:18–21 *or* Revelation 21:1–5a
Ministry of reconciliation:	2 Corinthians 5:17–18 *or* Matthew 5:43–48
Hope for the broken ones:	Matthew 5:1–12 *or* Psalm 51:15–17 *or* Isaiah 42:1–4
Dream of revolution:	Luke 1:46–53

E: *Honouring creation*

This section affirms the dependency of human life on the natural order, and of all things upon the creator. The theme may be connected with any of the following: environmental abuse, world hunger, natural disasters, climate change and the conserving and sharing of natural resources; aid agencies, environmentalists or global planning towards a sustainable future.

Celebrating creation:	Matthew 6:25–31 *or* Psalm 19:1–6 *or* Job 12:7–10
Stewardship of creation:	Genesis 1:26–31 *or* Psalm 8
Pollution:	Ezekiel 34:18–19 *or* Isaiah 24:4–6
Recycling:	John 6:11–13
Bio-diversity:	Genesis 7:12–16
Valuing water:	Exodus 17:1–6 *or* John 4:7–14
Valuing and sharing food:	Exodus 16:1–3, 13–18 *or* Mark 8:1–9

F: *Taking action for justice and peace*

This focuses on the translating of justice and peace concerns into action, and may include prayers for activists and campaigners, pressure groups

Extra Resources

and community projects, churches and public bodies, local and national politicians, those who are disempowered, those who prevent action taking place.

Action for justice and peace:	Matthew 25:34–36, 40 *or* Luke 4:16–21 *or* Luke 12:32–35 *or* Matthew 11:2–6
Action, not words:	Matthew 7:21–23 *or* Matthew 21:28–32
Worship/belief is not enough:	Isaiah 1:11–17 *or* Micah 6:6–8 *or* James 2:14–18
Called into action:	Exodus 3:7–8a, 4:10–16 *or* Luke 19:1–10
Those who prevent action:	Luke 11:37–47, 52–54

Songs *(familiar tunes, or easy to learn)*

Spirit of God, unseen as the wind

For the fruits of all creation (to: All through the night)

Sent by the Lord am I

How great thou art ('O Lord my God')

When I receive the peace of Christ

Touch the earth lightly

Jesus Christ is waiting

Inspired by love and anger

A touching place (Christ's is the world)

Says Jesus, come and gather round (to: Seven joys of Mary)

The Spirit lives to set us free

O Lord, all the world belongs to you

Make me a channel of your peace

Go tell everyone ('God's spirit is in my heart')

Kneels at the feet of his friends

Seek ye first the kingdom of God

We lay our broken world

Lord God, your love has called us here (to: Melita)

Kum ba ya

When I needed a neighbour

How good it is, what pleasure comes (to: Amazing grace)

Concluding prayers and blessing

After the song, the concluding prayers could consist of:

- *two or three one-line intercessions on the specific theme,*
- *followed by the prayer in the main order of service for the section A–F, read together and concluded with the blessing.*

Visual focus

A symbol may be placed on a small table to focus attention on the theme, such as: icons, paper chains, peace cranes for Hiroshima, fair trade coffee tin and mug, bowl and towel, Amnesty candle, contrasting meal portions, flowers, driftwood cross.

Actions

People's attention may be drawn to displays such as Amnesty International letter-writing sheets, fair trade produce lists or petitions. Or an opportunity may be given to light a candle, place a stone in water, attach a note to a cross, etc., as a sign of solidarity or commitment.

Extra Resources

THE IONA PILGRIMAGE

Over the centuries millions of pilgrims have come to this cradle of Christianity in Scotland, seeking healing, inspiration and new beginnings. And all have been received here, whether rich or poor, old or young.

Once a week everyone on Iona is welcome to join the pilgrimage around the island, visiting places of historical and religious significance and reflecting on the journey of our lives and the life of the world. At each station there is a brief reflection and prayer, and sometimes silence or songs.

The pilgrimage begins at 10.15 am at the foot of St Martin's Cross by the west door of the Abbey Church, and ends in St Oran's Chapel at approximately 4.00 pm. A packed lunch is provided for the guests of the Iona Community, and a cup of tea is provided for all at the Machair. Strong footwear and a warm waterproof coat are recommended. The pilgrimage path is often rough and wet underfoot. People may if they wish only do part of the day's journey, in which case it is simplest either to join us for the first half and depart after lunch, or arrive for lunch at the Machair (between 1.30 and 2.30 pm) for the second half.

St Martin's Cross has marked this place of pilgrimage for over a thousand years. It is named after St Martin, a fourth-century Roman soldier, who in sharing his clothing with a poor man received a vision of Christ. After his baptism he became known for his conscientious objection to serving in the Roman army, and later, as the Bishop of Tours, played an important role in the mission to the Celts. The high standing crosses of the Celtic Church suggest that worship often occurred out of doors in the midst of the power and beauty of creation: of earth, sea and sky. And the Celtic everlasting pattern of the weaving vine on the cross points to the intertwining of heaven and earth. Like others before him, George MacLeod, founder of the Iona Community, thought of the island as a very thin place, with little to separate spirit and matter. On our Iona pilgrimage we look for the spiritual at the heart of the physical world.

Bless to us, O God,

the earth beneath our feet.

Bless to us, O God,

the path whereon we go.

Bless to us, O God,

the people whom we meet.

Amen.

The Augustinian Nunnery was built around the same time as the 13th-century Benedictine Abbey. The Nunnery stands at the heart of the local community, surrounded by homes, school, clinic, library and village hall. Yet its ruins, sheltering carefully tended gardens, are peaceful as well as welcoming. We can imagine the nuns, worshipping in the nave of the little chapel, sharing meals in the refectory and meeting in their Chapter House. Yet there is in fact very little historical record of these women's lives. History has focused almost entirely on the Abbey. This echoes the way that, over the centuries, a male-dominated society and church has made women invisible. Their ministry was often in the home and local community – not in the places of power. Moreover, the subordination of women has often gone hand in hand with a neglect of the earth and an abuse of the human body.

Today some see the ancient Celtic Church as offering a greater balance between the feminine and masculine, as well as a celebration of the interweaving of matter and spirit, and an affirmation of the goodness of creation and the human body. St Brigid, for instance, in her leadership of double monasteries of men and women in the Celtic Church, stands for us as a model of equality between men and women.

Bless to us, O God,

our souls that come from on high.

Bless to us, O God,

our bodies that are of earth.

Bless to us, O God,

each thing our eyes see.

Bless to us, O God,

each sound our ears hear.

Bless to us, O God,

each odour that goes to our nostrils.

Bless to us, O God,

each taste that goes to our lips,

each note that goes to our song,

each ray that guides our way.

Amen.

The Marble Quarry, at the south-east corner of the island, is where the white Iona marble with green streaks of serpentine was quarried for the present-day communion table and baptismal font of the Abbey Church. The Benedictine high altar may have come from here too. Amid some of the oldest rock in the world, the marble quarry reminds us of earth's evolution over hundreds of millions of years, of our place in creation's history and our responsibility to care for the earth. The heaps of abandoned stone in the quarry remind us of the way we exploit the environment. We see this on a much larger scale elsewhere in the world. The cutting frame and engine also remind us of our working lives – the work that puts food on the table and uses human skills; the hard work that in the developing world is often poorly paid. In the marble quarry we reflect on the situations in our world where natural resources have been exploited, and where human lives have been broken and left in a heap in the pursuit of wealth and power; and here we give thanks for the goodness of creation, and for the ways we can be co-creators with God.

O Christ, there is no plant in the ground

but it is full of your virtue.

There is no form in the strand

but it is full of your blessing.

There is no life in the sea,

there is no creature in the ocean,

there is nothing in the heavens

but proclaims your goodness.

There is no bird on the wing,

there is no star in the sky,

there is nothing beneath the sun

but proclaims your goodness.

Amen.

St Columba's Bay is the pebbled beach at the southern tip of the island where Columba is said to have arrived from Ireland on Pentecost Sunday in the year 563. Legend has it that, having clambered up the beach with their leather-bound boat, known as a coracle, Columba and his twelve monks climbed the hill to the west of the bay to confirm that Ireland, their beloved home country, could not be seen. 'The Hill of Turning the Back to Ireland' became a landmark for them as they moved forward in mission. They established their monastic centre on the east side of the island around the present day site of the Abbey, and from there conducted a mission to the Picts in the north, to the Anglo-Saxons in Northumbria, and throughout Europe, reaching as far east as western Russia. St Columba's Bay is a place of leaving behind the past and of new beginnings in pilgrimage and mission.

And now, may kindly Columba guide you

to be an isle in the sea,

to be a hill on the shore,

to be a star in the night,

to be a staff for the weak.

Amen.

The Machair, which simply means 'raised beach', is the common land on the west side of the island overlooking the 'Bay at the Back of the Ocean'. For centuries it was used as the cornfield for the Celtic monastery and later by the Benedictines. The islanders also cultivated it, increasing the fertility with seaweed and hard work. The ridges of the lazy beds in the *runrig* system (a way of sharing land fairly) can still be seen. Now it is used in turn by the farmers for common grazing. So the Machair is like a parable of sharing, of co-operation as opposed to competition. Here we share our lunch together and give thanks, remembering that we are called to share the gifts of God with one another and with the poor of the world.

> Each thing we have received,
>
> from you it came, O God.
>
> Each thing for which we hope,
>
> from your love it will be given.
>
> Kindle in our hearts within
>
> a flame of love to our neighbours,
>
> to our foes, to our friends, to our loved ones all,
>
> from the lowliest thing that lives,
>
> to the name that is highest of all.
>
> Amen.

The Hermit's Cell, now only a secluded ring of stones, is situated towards the north of the island. These stones, which may be the remains of a sheepfold, possibly also mark the site of a Celtic beehive hut. Over the centuries this has been a place of solitude. There are accounts of Columba spending time alone in prayer on the island, and it may be that this was his place of hermitage. Times of solitude and silence undergird the busyness and demands of living interwoven in community. As well as hearing the word of God through the scriptures, through creation and through one another, we can experience the word of God deep within us, at the very heart of all being.

Deep peace of the running wave to you,

deep peace of the flowing air to you,

deep peace of the quiet earth to you,

deep peace of the shining stars to you,

deep peace of the Son of Peace to you.

Amen.

Dun I, which simply means the hill of Iona, is the highest point on the island, 102 metres above sea level. The pilgrimage may climb to the top, or pause at another high place. On a clear day one can see the Cuillins of Skye to the north, Ben More to the east, the Paps of Jura to the south, and the lighthouse of Skerryvore to the west, several miles off Tiree. Closer to the north lie the Treshnish Isles and the island of Staffa. At the north-eastern tip of the island is the White Strand of the Monks, where late in the 9th century the Abbot and fifteen monks were martyred. And earlier in that century at Martyrs' Bay sixty-eight monks had been slaughtered at the hands of Norse invaders. Iona, the holy island of peace, has known its own bloodshed and struggle.

In the biblical tradition, mountains or hills have been understood as places of new vision and transfiguration. Also in the Bible the sea is portrayed as a place of risk which can suddenly and unpredictably blow into storm. If Iona is like a hilltop experience of new perspective, then often the places that we return to are more like the dangerous seas. On Dun I we begin to refocus on those places of struggle in our world that we belong to and are aware of, and we offer a prayer for peace.

Peace between nations,

peace between neighbours,

peace between lovers,

in love of the God of life.

Peace between person and person,

peace between wife and husband,

peace between parent and child,

the peace of Christ above all peace.

Bless O Christ our faces,

let our faces bless everything.

Bless O Christ our eyes,

let our eyes bless all they see.

Amen.

St Oran's Chapel, in the island's graveyard, by the main gate of the Abbey grounds, is the oldest building on Iona. It was built in the twelfth century. Oran lived six centuries before and is remembered as the first Columban monk to die and be buried on Iona.

The area became known as the Reilig Oran (or the graveyard of Oran). Many Scottish kings and Lords of the Isles, as well as Irish and Norse kings, are said to be buried here. A graveyard may seem an odd place to end the Iona pilgrimage, but in the Christian Church we celebrate that it was in a graveyard that the resurrection faith began, and it is often in places of death and apparent hopelessness that new beginnings are given. Our prayer is that through the self-giving and deaths of Oran and Columba and the many other women and men who have gone before us we may be granted the strength and vision to continue on the journey of Jesus.

May God be a bright flame before you,

be a guiding star above you,

be a smooth path below you,

be a kindly shepherd behind you,

today, tomorrow and for ever.

Amen.

GENERAL WORSHIP RESOURCES

RESPONSES, PRAYERS AND SONGS

A. RESPONSES

In the beginning

Leader: In the beginning,

when it was very dark,

God said, 'Let there be light'

ALL: AND THERE WAS LIGHT.

(The sign of light –

a lighted candle is placed on a central table)

Leader: In the beginning,

when it was very quiet,

the Word was with God

ALL: AND WHAT GOD WAS, THE WORD WAS.

(The sign of the Word –

an open Bible is placed on the table)

Leader: When the time was right

God sent the Son.

ALL: HE CAME AMONG US,

HE WAS ONE OF US.

(The sign of the Son –

a cross is placed on the table)

Hope for the world

Leader: In quietness and darkness,

in peace and confusion,

Jesus Christ wants to make his home

and meet his friends.

He is the light of life:

ALL: HE IS THE HOPE FOR THE WORLD.

Leader: In him there is neither Jew nor Gentile,

neither Roman Catholic nor Protestant,

ALL: ALL ARE ONE IN JESUS CHRIST.

Leader: He is the light of life:

ALL: HE IS THE HOPE OF THE WORLD.

Leader: In him there is neither black nor white,

neither north nor south:

ALL: ALL ARE ONE IN JESUS CHRIST.

Leader: He is the light of life:

ALL: HE IS THE HOPE OF THE WORLD.

Leader: In him there is neither male nor female,

neither master nor servant:

ALL: ALL ARE ONE IN JESUS CHRIST.

Leader: He is the light of life:

ALL: HE IS THE HOPE FOR THE WORLD.

Leader: In him there is neither rich nor poor,

neither middle class nor working class:

ALL:	ALL ARE ONE IN JESUS CHRIST.
Leader:	He is the light of life:
ALL:	HE IS THE HOPE FOR THE WORLD.

Made in love

Leader:	In the beginning, God made the world,
ALL:	MADE IN LOVE FOR MAN AND WOMAN;
Leader:	The earth was filled with lovely things,
ALL:	MADE IN LOVE FOR MAN AND WOMAN;
Leader:	Out of the dust God made new creatures,
ALL:	MADE IN LOVE FOR MAN AND WOMAN;
Leader:	These, God said, were in God's image,
ALL:	MADE IN LOVE FOR MAN AND WOMAN;
Leader:	And to the world there came God's Son,
ALL:	KING OF LOVE, FOR MAN AND WOMAN.

When the lights are on

Leader:	When the lights are on
	and the house is full
	and laughter is easy
	and all is well …
Voice:	Behold I stand at the door and knock.
Leader:	When the lights are low
	and the house is still
	and the talk is intense
	and the air is full of wondering …
Voice:	Behold I stand at the door and knock.

Leader: When the lights are off

and the house is sad

and the voice is troubled

and nothing seems right …

Voice: Behold I stand at the door and knock.

Leader: And tonight,

always tonight,

as if there were no other people,

no other house,

no other door …

Voice: Behold I stand at the door and knock.

Leader: Come, Lord Jesus, be our guest,

stay with us for the day is ending.

Bring to our house your poverty,

ALL: FOR THEN SHALL WE BE RICH.

Leader: Bring to our house your pain,

ALL: THAT SHARING IT WE MAY ALSO SHARE YOUR JOY.

Leader: Bring to our house your understanding of us,

ALL: THAT WE MAY BE FREED TO LEARN MORE OF YOU.

Leader: Bring to our house all those

who hurry or hirple (hobble) behind you,

ALL: THAT WE MAY MEET YOU AS THE SAVIOUR OF ALL.

Leader: Bring to our house your Holy Spirit,

ALL: THAT THIS MAY BE A CRADLE OF LOVE.

Leader: With friend, with stranger,

with neighbour, and the well-known ones,

be among us tonight,

ALL: FOR THE DOORS OF OUR HOUSE WE OPEN

AND THE DOORS OF OUR HEARTS WE LEAVE AJAR.

The sun rises

Leader: The sun rises and it is light, night falls and it is dark.

ALL: BLESS THE ONE WHO GIVES THE LIFE.

<u>Men:</u>   Sow the seed and cut the corn;

<u>Women:</u>   Bear the child and build the house;

ALL: BLESS THE ONE WHO GIVES THE LIFE.

<u>Men:</u>   Lay the stone and light the fire;

<u>Women:</u>   Cast the net and water the earth;

ALL: BLESS THE ONE WHO GIVES THE LIFE.

<u>Men:</u>   Serve the guest and pay the price;

<u>Women:</u>   Nail the wood and pick the flowers;

ALL: BLESS THE ONE WHO GIVES THE LIFE.

<u>Men:</u>   Make the wine and bake the bread;

<u>Women:</u>   Pour the wine and break the bread;

ALL: BLESS THE ONE WHO GIVES THE LIFE.

Witnesses for peace

Leader: Sisters and brothers in Jesus Christ,

let us call to mind and to be present with us

those who have lived, worked, spoken

and witnessed for peace

in this and other ages.

Jesus Christ, Prince of Peace …

ALL: STAND WITH US NOW.

Leader: Mary Magdalene, witness to the resurrection …
ALL: STAND WITH US NOW.

Leader: Paul of Tarsus, Apostle of Peace …
ALL: STAND WITH US NOW.

(At this point, throughout the Abbey, people may mention a name or names of those who have inspired them on issues of justice and peace. After stating the name, they say, 'STAND WITH US NOW.' They rise on speaking and others around them who want to be associated with that name stand also, e.g. 'Francis of Assisi … STAND WITH US NOW.')

(After names have been called, the leader will proceed:)

Leader: All you who have died in war

            since the war to end all wars …
ALL: STAND WITH US NOW.

Leader: All you who tread the path of peace …
ALL: STAND WITH US NOW.

Leader: Sisters and brothers in Jesus Christ,

            let us stand in silence,

            for the world is worried

            and the Prince of Peace is moving towards a cross.

            (Silence)

Leader: Do not be afraid … says Jesus,

            I have overcome the world.

            The peace I give, the world will never take away.

We call on the power of God

Leader: We call on the power of God
        to meet us in our helplessness:

ALL: GOD IN OUR THINKING, GOD IN OUR SPEAKING.

Leader: We call on the clarity of God
        to meet us in our confusion:

ALL: GOD IN OUR ACTING, GOD IN OUR STILLNESS.

Leader: We call on the mercy of God
        to meet us in our brokenness:

ALL: GOD IN OUR WAKING, GOD IN OUR SLEEPING.

Leader: We call on the Spirit of God to meet us in our division:

ALL: GOD IN OUR MEETING, GOD IN OUR PARTING.

The kingdom of God

(These three litanies have a common theme but are included for use separately. A fourth litany, originally called 'Power to choose', forms the opening responses in the Agape.)

Power to change

Leader: Out of judgement came mercy

ALL: AND GOD DID NOT ABANDON THE PEOPLE,

Men: For the love that God bore them, coming again,

Women: For the hope that God had for them, bearing their pain.

Leader: Out of gentleness came strength

ALL: AND GOD SPOKE A WORD:

Men: To the outcast and stranger, making them welcome,

Women: To the sick and despairing, making them whole.

Leader:	Out of freedom came faithfulness
ALL:	AND GOD DIED ON THE CROSS:
<u>*Men:*</u>	For the poor and the prisoner, the sign of deliverance;
<u>*Women:*</u>	For God loved the world so much
	that he gave his only Son
ALL:	THAT EVERYONE WHO BELIEVES IN HIM MAY NOT DIE,
	BUT HAVE ETERNAL LIFE.

Power to love   *5. 3. 09*

Leader:	Out of death came life
ALL:	AND GOD DEFEATED EVIL:
<u>*Men:*</u>	An empty cross and an empty tomb,
<u>*Women:*</u>	A nail mark shown and a presence known.
Leader:	Out of sorrow came joy
ALL:	AND GOD SENT THE SPIRIT:
<u>*Men:*</u>	Coming like fire to all people and ages,
<u>*Women:*</u>	Coming to birth in the water of life.
Leader:	Out of difference came unity
ALL:	AND GOD'S PEOPLE WERE CALLED:
<u>*Men:*</u>	Called to receive him in bread and wine,
<u>*Women:*</u>	Called to be free in the power of love.
Leader:	For when the Holy Spirit comes upon you,
	you will be filled with power
ALL:	AND BE WITNESSES FOR CHRIST
	TO THE ENDS OF THE EARTH.

God's power shown

Leader:	Out of love comes celebration
ALL:	AND GOD'S KINGDOM IS AMONG US:
Men:	Where peace is the means of making us one,
Women:	Where truth does not stumble and justice is done.

Leader:	Out of change comes possibility
ALL:	AND GOD'S NEW CREATION IS BEGUN:
Men:	Promise of splendour and signal of worth,
Women:	Source of all goodness, renewing the earth.

Leader:	Out of freedom comes responsibility
ALL:	AND GOD CALLS US TO DISCIPLESHIP:
Men:	In our compassion, making love known,
Women:	In our conviction, God's power shown.
Leader:	You did not choose me, I chose you.
ALL:	THIS, THEN, IS WHAT I COMMAND YOU:
	LOVE ONE ANOTHER.

Blessing the world

(The order may be varied, and other names and phrases used, as appropriate)

Leader: People of Ireland,

            torn and tired of being torn …

ALL: GOD'S PEACE IS FOR YOU.

Leader: People of Africa,

            exploited and tired of being exploited …

ALL: GOD'S PEACE IS FOR YOU.

Leader: People of the Middle East,

            turbulent and tired of being turbulent …

ALL: GOD'S PEACE IS FOR YOU

Leader: People of South America,

            silenced and tired of being silenced …

ALL: GOD'S PEACE IS FOR YOU.

Leader: People of India,

            divided and tired of being divided …

ALL: GOD'S PEACE IS FOR YOU.

Leader: People of Eastern Europe,

            anxious and tired of being anxious …

ALL: GOD'S PEACE IS FOR YOU.

Leader: People of the West,

            privileged and tired of being privileged …

ALL: GOD'S PEACE IS FOR YOU.

Leader:	May the God of all people and the Lord Jesus Christ
	give us grace and peace this night and every night.
ALL:	AMEN.

God of life *4. 26. 09*

Leader:	O God of life, of all life and of each life,
	we lay our lives before you.
	We give our lives to you,
	from whom nothing in us is hidden.
Women:	You are before us, God, you are behind;
Men:	You are around us, God, you are within.

Leader:	O God of life,
	you know the secret thoughts of every heart.
Women:	We bring the faith that is in us, and the doubt;
Men:	We bring the joy that is in us, and the sorrow.

Leader:	O God of life, you are in the light, and in the darkness.
Women:	We bring the knowledge that is in us, and the ignorance;
Men:	We bring the hope that is in us, and the despair.

Leader:	O God of life, O generous Spirit,
ALL:	RENEW US WITH YOUR LIFE,
	TONIGHT, TOMORROW AND ALWAYS. AMEN.

The cross

Leader: The cross …

ALL: WE SHALL TAKE IT.

Leader: The bread …

ALL: WE SHALL BREAK IT.

Leader: The pain …

ALL: WE SHALL BEAR IT.

Leader: The joy …

ALL: WE SHALL SHARE IT.

Leader: The gospel …

ALL: WE SHALL LIVE IT.

Leader: The love …

ALL: WE SHALL GIVE IT.

Leader: The light …

ALL: WE SHALL CHERISH IT.

Leader: The darkness …

ALL: GOD SHALL PERISH IT.

   AMEN.

B. PRAYERS

Make us one

Leader: O Trinity of love,

God in community,

holy and one,

look now on us

who look to you …

ALL: AND HEAR OUR PRAYER FOR OUR COMMUNITY:

Leader: Where there is falseness …

ALL: SMOTHER IT BY YOUR TRUTH;

Leader: Where there is any coldness …

ALL: KINDLE THE FLAME OF YOUR LOVE;

Leader: Where there is joy and hope …

ALL: FREE US TO SHARE IT TOGETHER;

Leader: And make us one …

ALL: AS YOU ARE ONE.

Leader: Before God and you who are near me,

I release anything I hold against you;

I regret all I have done to harm you;

I stand beside the wrong in my life

and ask for God's forgiveness.

ALL: BEFORE GOD AND YOU WHO ARE NEAR,

WE RELEASE ANYTHING WE HOLD

AGAINST ONE ANOTHER;

WE REGRET ALL THE HARM WE HAVE DONE;

WE STAND BESIDE THE WRONG IN OUR LIVES
AND ASK FOR GOD'S FORGIVENESS.

(Silence)

Leader: Jesus says to us, each one:
'Go and sin no more,
 come and follow me.'
Now bind our hands with honesty
as we offer them to each other
and our prayer to you: *(join hands if appropriate)*

ALL: OUR FATHER IN HEAVEN,
HALLOWED BE YOUR NAME;
YOUR KINGDOM COME, YOUR WILL BE DONE,
ON EARTH AS IT IS IN HEAVEN.
GIVE US TODAY OUR DAILY BREAD.
FORGIVE US OUR SINS
AS WE FORGIVE THOSE WHO SIN AGAINST US.
SAVE US IN THE TIME OF TRIAL
AND DELIVER US FROM EVIL.
FOR THE KINGDOM, THE POWER AND THE GLORY
ARE YOURS,
NOW AND FOR EVER. AMEN.

Early in the morning

Leader: O God,
early in the morning,
when the world was young,
you made life in all its beauty and terror;

	you gave birth to all that we know.
ALL:	HALLOWED BE YOUR NAME.

Leader:	Early in the morning,
	when the world least expected it,
	a new born child crying in a cradle
	announced that you had come among us,
	that you were one of us.
ALL:	HALLOWED BE YOUR NAME.

Leader:	Early in the morning,
	surrounded by self-interested religious leaders,
	anxious statesmen
	and silent friends,
	you accepted the penalty for doing good,
	for being God:
	you shouldered and suffered the cross.
ALL:	HALLOWED BE YOUR NAME.

Leader:	Early in the morning,
	a voice in a guarded graveyard
	and footsteps in the dew
	proved that you had risen,
	that you had come back
	to those and for those
	who had forgotten, denied and destroyed you.
ALL:	O GOD, BRING NEW LIFE
	WHERE WE ARE WORN AND TIRED,
	NEW LOVE
	WHERE WE HAVE TURNED HARD-HEARTED,

FORGIVENESS
WHERE WE HAVE WOUNDED,
AND THE JOY AND FREEDOM OF YOUR HOLY SPIRIT
WHERE WE ARE THE PRISONERS OF OUR SELVES.

(Silence)

Leader: To all and to each,

where regret is real,

God pronounces pardon

and grants us the right to begin again.

Thanks be to God!

ALL: AMEN.

The gospel of the God of life

The gospel of the God of life to shelter us:

the gospel of the God of life to help us,

to keep us from all malice, to keep us from all anguish.

Christ himself is shepherd over us,

enfolding us on every side.

He will not leave us forsaken, nor let evil come near us.

The blessing of the God of life

The blessing of the God of life be ours,

the blessing of the loving Christ be ours,

the blessing of the Holy Spirit be ours,

to cherish us, to help us, to make us holy.

May God's goodness be yours

May God's goodness be yours,

and well, and seven times well, may you spend your lives:

may you be an isle in the sea,

may you be a hill on the shore,

may you be a star in the darkness,

may you be a staff to the weak;

may the love Christ Jesus gave fill every heart for you;

may the love Christ Jesus gave fill you for every one.

God of life, do not darken your light

God of life, do not darken your light to us,

O God of life, do not close your joy to us,

O God of life, do not shut your door to us,

O God of life, do not refuse your mercy to us,

and, O God of life, crown us with your gladness.

O God, open to us today

O God, open to us today the sea of your mercy

and water us with full streams

from the riches of your grace

and springs of your kindness.

Make us children of quietness and heirs of peace:

kindle in us the fire of your love;

sow in us your fear;

strengthen our weakness by your power

and bind us close to you and to each other.

Christ stands before you

Christ stands before you, and peace is in his mind.

Sleep in the calm of all calm,

sleep in the guidance of all guidance,

sleep in the love of all loves:

sleep, beloved, in the God of life.

O God, give us your shielding

O God, give us your shielding,

O God, give us your holiness,

O God, give us your comfort

and your peace at the hour of our death.

O God, our Creator

O God, our Creator,

your kindness has brought us the gift of a new day.

Help us to leave yesterday,

and not to covet tomorrow,

but to accept the uniqueness of today.

Christ, draw near to us

Christ, draw near to us,

little people, trembling and most wretched,

rowing through the infinite storm

of this age;

and bring us safely

to the most beautiful haven of life.

(Based on words attributed to St Columba)

My Christ, my shield

My Christ, my shield, my encircler,

each day, each night, each light, each dark,

be near me, uphold me, my treasure, my triumph.

As you have been fed

As you have been fed at this table

go to feed the hungry.

As you have been set free

go to set free the imprisoned.

As you have received – give.

As you have heard – proclaim.

And the blessing which you have received

from Creator, Son and Spirit

go with you.

O my soul's healer

O my soul's healer, keep me at evening;

keep me at morning, keep me at noon.

I am tired, astray and stumbling.

Shield me from sin.

God to enfold us

God to enfold us, God to surround us;

God in our speaking, God in our thinking;

God in our life, God on our lips;

God in our souls, God in our hearts.

C. SONGS

MORNING AND EVENING, WELCOME AND GATHERING, JUSTICE AND PEACE

MORNING SONGS OF PRAISE

God's graceful moment

(Set to *Picardy*, Church Hymnary 3, no. 577)

1. Morning opens wide before us
    like a door into the light.
    Just beyond, the day lies waiting
    ready to throw off the night,
    and we stand upon its threshold
    poised to turn and take its flight.

2. Now the earth in all its glory
    springs to meet the rising sun,
    warms to all who walk upon it,
    cradling all that will be done.
    All our labour, all our loving
    mingle and become as one.

3. We receive God's graceful moment,
    while the day is fresh and still,
    ours to choose how we will greet it,
    ours to make it what we will.
    Here is given perfect freedom,
    every hope in love to fulfil.

4. As we take the first step together,
    passing through the door of the day,

may the love of Christ the Creator

give us peace in all that we say,

heart for all that lies before us,

grace to guide us on our way.

Today I awake

1.   Today I awake

and God is before me.

At night, as I dreamt,

he summoned the day;

for God never sleeps

but patterns the morning

with slivers of gold

or glory in grey.

2.   Today I arise

and Christ is beside me.

He walked through the dark

to scatter new light.

Yes, Christ is alive,

and beckons his people

to hope and to heal,

resist and invite.

3.   Today I affirm

the Spirit within me

at worship and work,

in struggle and rest.

The Spirit inspires

all life which is changing
from fearing to faith,
from broken to blest.

4.   Today I enjoy
the Trinity round me,
above and beneath,
before and behind;
the Maker, the Son,
the Spirit together
they called me to life
and call me their friend.

Oh the life of the world

1.   Oh the life of the world is a joy and a treasure,
unfolding in beauty the green-growing tree,
the changing of seasons in mountain and valley
the stars and the bright restless sea.

2.   Oh the life of the world is a fountain of goodness
overflowing in labour and passion and pain,
in the sound of the city and the silence of wisdom,
in the birth of a child once again.

3.   Oh the life of the world is the source of our healing.
It rises in laughter and wells up in song;
it springs from the care of the poor and the broken
and refreshes where justice is strong.

4.   So give thanks for the life and give love to the Maker
      and rejoice in the gift of the bright risen Son.
      And walk in the peace and the power of the Spirit
      till the days of our living are done.

Enemy of apathy

1.   She sits like a bird, brooding on the waters,
      hovering on the chaos of the world's first day;
      she sighs and she sings, mothering creation,
      waiting to give birth to all the Word will say.

2.   She wings over earth, resting where she wishes,
      lighting close at hand or soaring through the skies;
      she nests in the womb, welcoming each wonder,
      nourishing potential hidden to our eyes.

3.   She dances in fire, startling her spectators,
      waking tongues of ecstasy where dumbness reigned;
      she weans and inspires all whose hearts are open,
      nor can she be captured, silenced or restrained.

4.   For she is the Spirit, one with God in essence,
      gifted by the Saviour in eternal love;
      she is the key opening the scriptures,
      enemy of apathy and heavenly dove.

Dance and sing

Chorus: DANCE AND SING, ALL THE EARTH,

GRACIOUS IS THE HAND THAT TENDS YOU;

LOVE AND CARE EVERYWHERE,

GOD ON PURPOSE SENDS YOU.

1. Shooting star and sunset shape the drama of creation,

lightning flash and moonbeam share a common derivation.

2. Deserts stretch and torrents roar in contrast and confusion,

tree tops shake and mountains soar and nothing is illusion.

3. All that flies and swims and crawls displays an animation,

none can emulate or change for each has its own station.

4. Brother man and sister woman, born of dust and passion,

praise the one who calls us friends and makes us in like fashion.

5. Kiss of life and touch of death suggest our imperfection;

crib and womb and cross and tomb cry out for resurrection.

Christ be beside me

1. Christ be beside me,

Christ be before me,

Christ be behind me,

king of my heart.

Christ be within me,

Christ be below me,

Christ be above me,

never to part.

2.   Christ on my right hand,
       Christ on my left hand,
       Christ all around me,
       shield in the strife.
       Christ in my sleeping,
       Christ in my sitting,
       Christ in my rising,
       light of my life.

3.   Christ be in all hearts
       thinking about me,
       Christ be in all tongues
       telling of me.
       Christ be the vision
       in eyes that see me,
       in ears that hear me,
       Christ ever be.

Sing for God's glory

1.   Sing for God's glory that colours the dawn of creation,
       racing across the sky trailing bright clouds of elation;
       sun of delight succeeds the velvet of night,
       warming the earth's exultation.

2.   Sing for God's power that shatters the chains that would bind us,
       searing the darkness of fear and despair that could blind us,
       touching our shame with love that will not lay blame,
       reaching out gently to find us.

3.   Sing for God's justice disturbing each easy illusion,

       tearing down tyrants and putting our pride to confusion;

       lifeblood of right, resisting evil and slight,

       offering freedom's transfusion.

4.   Sing for God's saints who have travelled faith's journey before us,

       who, in our weariness, give us their hope to restore us;

       in them we see the new creation to be,

       Spirit of love made flesh for us.

I owe my Lord a morning song

1.   I owe my Lord a morning song

       for God has meant this day.

       Through fears of night and hidden light

       God moves and wills my way.

2.   I owe my Lord a morning song

       for Jesus rose at dawn;

       he made death die and would not lie

       that others might live on.

3.   I owe my Lord a morning song;

       the Spirit gave me voice,

       nor did she force my soul to praise

       but honoured me with choice.

4.   I owe my Lord a morning song.

       How can I help but sing

       when God is all in all,

       and I am one with everything.

Humbly in your sight

1.   Humbly in your sight we come together, Lord:
      grant us now the blessing of your presence here.

2.   These, our hearts, are yours; we give them to you, Lord:
      purify your love to make it like your own.

3.   These, our eyes, are yours; we give them to you, Lord:
      may we always see your world as with your sight.

4.   These, our hands, are yours; we give them to you, Lord;
      give them strength and skill to do our work for you.

5.   These, our feet, are yours; we give them to you, Lord:
      may we walk along the path of life with you.

6.   These, our tongues, are yours; we give them to you, Lord:
      may we speak your healing words of life and truth.

7.   These, our ears, are yours; we give them to you, Lord:
      open them to hear your words of guidance, Lord.

8.   Our whole selves are yours; we give them to you, Lord:
      take us now and keep us yours for evermore.

I will always bless the Lord

1.   I will always bless the Lord,
      praise his name and love his word.
      Humble folk will fill with joy,
      as in God I glory.

2. When I prayed God answered me,
    from my fears he set me free;
    none who trust God's faithful love
    shall be disappointed.

3. Those who cry are listened to,
    those in need receive their due:
    angels guard God's loyal folk,
    keeping them from danger.

4. Taste and see that God is good,
    know your yearnings understood,
    find your true security,
    be God's holy people.

5. Alleluia, alleluia, alleluia, alleluia.

SONGS FOR GATHERING

The God of heaven

Chorus: THE GOD OF HEAVEN IS PRESENT ON EARTH
    IN WORD AND SILENCE AND SHARING,
    IN FACE OF DOUBT, IN DEPTH OF FAITH,
    IN SIGNS OF LOVE AND CARING.

1. Gentler than air, wilder than wind,
    settling yet also deranging,
    the Spirit thrives on human lives,
    both changeless and yet changing.

2.   Far from the church, outside the fold,
     where prayer turns feeble and nervous,
     the Spirit wills society's ills
     be healed through humble service.

3.   From rural quiet to urban riot,
     in every social confusion,
     the Spirit pleads for all that leads
     to freedom from illusion.

4.   Truth after tears, trust after fears,
     God leaving everyone wiser,
     the Spirit springs through hopeless things
     transforming what defies her.

A SONG FOR THE WELCOME SERVICE

(See also the list in Extra Resources for the Welcome Service)

The love of God comes close

1.   The love of God comes close
     where stands an open door
     to let the stranger in,
     to mingle rich and poor:
     the love of God is here to stay,
     embracing those who walk his way.

2.   The peace of God comes close
     to those caught in the storm,
     forgoing lives of ease,

to ease the lives forlorn:
the peace of God is here to stay,
embracing those who walk his way.

3.   The joy of God comes close
where faith encounters fears,
where heights and depths of life
are found through smiles and tears:
the joy of God is here to stay,
embracing those who walk his way.

4.   The grace of God comes close
to those whose grace is spent,
when hearts are tired or sore
and hope is bruised or bent:
the grace of God is here to stay,
embracing those who walk his way.

SONGS FOR EVENING

Night has fallen

Leader: Night has fallen,
ALL: NIGHT HAS FALLEN,
           GRACIOUS SPIRIT, GUARD US SLEEPING.

Leader: Darkness now has come,
ALL: DARKNESS NOW HAS COME,
           GRACIOUS SPIRIT, GUARD US SLEEPING.

Leader: We are with you, God,

ALL: WE ARE WITH YOU, GOD,

             GRACIOUS SPIRIT, GUARD US SLEEPING.

Leader: See your children, God,

ALL: SEE YOUR CHILDREN, GOD,

             GRACIOUS SPIRIT, GUARD US SLEEPING.

Leader: Keep us in your love,

ALL: KEEP US IN YOUR LOVE,

             GRACIOUS SPIRIT, GUARD US SLEEPING.

Leader: Now we go to rest,

ALL: NOW WE GO TO REST,

             GRACIOUS SPIRIT, GUARD US SLEEPING,

             GRACIOUS SPIRIT, GUARD US SLEEPING.

Thank you for the night

1.   Thank you for the night,
     the sign that day is done,
     that life is meant to rest
     and sleep to come.

2.   Thank you for the quiet
     as silence scatters sound,
     while God, in both,
     is waiting to be found.

3.   Thank you for the dark
     to complement the light,
     as insight, open-eyed,
     replaces sight.

4.   Thank you for the word,

which darkness can't contain,

that life, laid down,

is raised to life again.

5.   Thank you for the night,

a measure of your care.

In darkness, as in light,

you, Lord, are there.

Now that evening falls

1.   Now that evening falls,

gently fades the light;

moon replaces sun

and day takes leave of night.

2.   Gratitude we raise

for the day that's gone

and for love that stays

till dusk is kissed by dawn.

3.   To the Maker's care

we in faith commend

all we love and long for,

all we still intend.

4.   Glory be to God,

glory to the Son,

glory to the Spirit,

ever three in one.

Let us stay together for a time

1. Let us stay together for a time

    let us stay together for a while

    when the evening is approaching

    and the day is almost spent

    let us stay with one another for a time.

    All we have in common is a road;

    all we have in common is a journey:

    we are simply fellow travellers

    who are passing in the night

    let us stay with one another on the road

    for a time.

2. Dare we trust a stranger with our dreams?

    Dare we trust a stranger with our story?

    If we cannot hide our tears

    let us share our hopes and fears

    as we stay with one another, with our dreams.

    All we have to offer is our Word;

    all we have to offer is a Bible

    let us open it between us

    till the fire burns within us,

    as we stay with one another in the Word

    for a time.

3. He was nothing to us but a name,

    and we thought our road would never find him

    he was with us all the while

and he's walking every mile
as we stay with one another in his name.

All we have between us is a loaf;
all we have between us is a table:
as we break the bread together
we will recognise our brother,
and we'll stay with one another, breaking bread,
for a time.

4. Shall we stay for ever in this place?
Shall we go back home and tell the others?
If we stay on holy ground
we'll lose the miracle we've found
and we'll be left with one another in this place.

We don't need a special place or time;
we don't have to travel to Emmaus:
any road and any table
we can meet you, Lord, again;
we can stay with one another any place,
any time.

Nears the ending of the day

Chorus

Choir: Nears the ending of the day;
sleep and shadows find their way;

ALL: TURNS THE WORLD BY GOD'S OWN HAND;
COMES THE NIGHT TO REST THE LAND.

1. *Solo:*   Praise the Maker of all time and space,
              never bound to one insight or place.
   ALL: PRAISE THE MAKER OF ALL TIME AND SPACE,
             NEVER BOUND TO ONE INSIGHT OR PLACE.

   Chorus: *(as before)*

2. *Solo:*   Praise the Maker of all things that move,
             held, yet liberated, by God's love.
   ALL: *(repeat)*

3. *Solo:*   Praise the Maker of the day that's done,
             even now preparing light to come.
   ALL: *(repeat)*

4. *Solo:*   Praise the Maker, praise the Maker's Son,
             praise the Spirit binding all in one.
   ALL: *(repeat)*

Stay with us now

1. *Cantor:*   Day is almost ended:
   ALL: JESUS CHRIST, LORD OF ALL,
               STAY WITH US NOW.

2.   Find your way among us:

3.   Listen to the anxious:

4.   Sit beside the lonely:

5.   Contradict the callous:

6.   Comfort and disturb us:

7. Do not ever leave us:

8. Even when we doubt you:

9. Maker of tomorrow:

10.. Keep us through the darkness:

JUSTICE AND PEACE SONGS

When our Lord walked the earth

1. When our Lord walked the earth
    all the world found its worth;
    as declared at his birth,
    God became our neighbour,
    granting with his favour.

    POWER TO SPEAK AND HEAL,
    GRACE TO KNOW WHAT'S REAL,
    WISDOM, INSIGHT AND FAITH,
    LOVE AND UNDERSTANDING.

2. Through his life, through his death,
    through each gesture and breath,
    Jesus joined faith and deed,
    model for our caring,
    showing and yet sharing.

3. Jesus loves all his friends,
    and that love never ends.
    To his Church gifts he sends
    through the Holy Spirit;
    these we shall inherit.

4.   Sing aloud and rejoice,

clap your hands, raise your voice,

for with unnerving choice

God in love has found us,

and displays around us …

There is a line of women   *5.10.09*

1.   There is a line of women,

extending back to Eve,

whose role in shaping history

God only could conceive.

And though, through endless ages,

their witness was repressed,

God valued and encouraged them

through whom the world was blessed.

So sing a song of Sarah

to laughter she gave birth;

and sing a song of Tamar

who stood for women's worth;

and sing a song of Hannah

who bargained with her Lord;

and sing a song of Mary

who bore and bred God's Word.

2.   There is a line of women

who took on powerful men,

defying laws and scruples

to let life live again.

And though, despite their triumph,

their stories stayed untold
God kept their number growing,
creative, strong and bold.

So sing a song of Shiphrah
with Puah at her hand,
engaged to kill male children
they foiled the king's command.
And sing a song of Rahab
who sheltered spies and lied;
and sing a song of Esther,
preventing genocide.

3.   There is a line of women
who stood by Jesus' side,
who housed him while he ministered
and held him when he died.
And though they claimed he'd risen
their news was deemed suspect
till Jesus stood among them,
his womanly elect.

So sing a song of Anna
who saw Christ's infant face;
and sing a song of Martha
who gave him food and space;
and sing of all the Marys
who heeded his requests,
and now at heaven's banquet
are Jesus' fondest guests.

To be a soldier

1. To be a soldier,

   to fight for peace till war shall end

   this is the conflict

   Christ calls you to attend:

   to forfeit safety for danger,

   make room for the stranger,

   turn enemy to friend.

2. To be a soldier,

   prepare to wage a cosmic fight:

   the strength of armies

   is not the only might.

   Sin must be stripped from high places;

   what scars souls and faces

   must die through truth and light.

3. To be a soldier,

   do more than wish that wars would cease;

   expose injustice,

   procure the slaves' release;

   then enter politics praying,

   and break rank obeying

   the power and Prince of peace

4. Think not to weary

   nor lay your great commission down,

   nor crave approval,

   nor fear the critics' word

Prevail through fears, love with laughter,

risk all, then hereafter

return to Christ your sword.

PSALMS

Psalms in a six week cycle

Weeks	I	II	III	IV	V	VI
Monday (Justice & peace themes)	10	37	72	82	98	146
Tuesday (Healing themes)	30	42	46	63	130	142
Wednesday (Commitment themes)	22	34	40	51	119	145
Thursday (Communion themes)	84	91	96	111	133	138
Friday (Leaving themes)	16	18	23	121	126	139
Saturday (Creation and Welcome)	8	19	29	65	104	148

The translation of the following psalms seeks to be faithful to the texts.
Clarity, inclusive language, and appropriateness for worship and the daily
themes are aided by selection of verses and occasional paraphrasing.

PSALMS

Psalm 8

ALL: WONDERFUL GOD, CREATOR,
              THE WHOLE EARTH DECLARES YOUR GREATNESS.

A: Your glory glows in the heavens.
              It is babbled by babies and sung by children.

B: You are safe from all your enemies:
              those who oppose you are silenced.

A: When I look at the sky which you have made,
              the moon and the stars that you set in place:

B: Where do human beings fit in the pattern?
              What are we, that you care for us?

A: You have made us only a little lower than yourself;
              and crowned us with glory and honour.

B: You share with us responsibility
              to care for sheep and cattle, wild things, birds and fish,
              everything that lives in the sea:
              to work with you, within creation.

ALL: WONDERFUL GOD, CREATOR,
              THE WHOLE EARTH DECLARES YOUR GREATNESS.

Psalm 10

A: Why do you stand aloof, O God?
        Why hide when troubles come?

B: In arrogance the wicked oppress the poor,
        and catch them in schemes they devise.

A: Proudly they boast of their desires;
        greedy for profit, they curse you.
        Contemptuous of all your ways,
        they say, There is no God!

B: They scoff at whoever opposes them;
        they think they cannot fail.

A: They lie in wait among the reeds
        to bring down the innocent by stealth.

B: Their eyes watch out for the helpless;
        they lurk like lions in their den.

A: They lurk in hiding to seize the poor,
        to seize and drag them away.

B: They think you will forget.
        They think you do not see.

A: Arise, O God! Lift up your hand!
        Do not forget the oppressed.
        Why should the wicked spurn you
        and imagine you will not act?   ▶

B: You do see! This misery and suffering

       you take into your hands.

       The helpless entrust themselves to you;

       you come to the aid of the poor.

A: Break the strength of the evildoer;

       search out wickedness till you find none.

       Give strength, instead, to the hearts of the poor

       as you listen to their laments.

B: Give a hearing to the orphaned and the oppressed;

       restore their rights, O God,

       so that those who live upon the earth

       may strike terror in them no more.

ALL: AMEN.

Psalm 16

A: Protect me, O God; in you I am safe.

       I say to you, You are my God;

       only from you comes the good I enjoy.

B: How excellent are your faithful people!

       It is my greatest pleasure to be with them.

A: Those who idolise lesser things bring trouble upon themselves.

       I will not take part in their practices, nor worship their gods.

B: You, O God, are all I have, and you give me all I need;

       my future is in your hands.

A: I praise you, for you are my guide;

and by night you speak to my conscience.

B: I am always aware of your presence:

so near that nothing can shake me.

A: So my heart is glad, and my soul delights;

my body can rest secure.

B: You will not leave me to the world of the dead,

nor banish to the abyss one whom you love.

A: You will show me the path to life.

Your presence will be my unbounded joy,

my delight for ever more.

ALL: AMEN.

Psalm 18

A: How I love you, God, my strength,

my rock, my fortress, my champion.

B: You are the rock where I take refuge;

my shield, my sure defender;

my stronghold and my shelter

A: In the anguish of my heart, O God,

I called to you for help.

From your sanctuary you heard my voice;

my cry came to your ears.   ▶

B: You reached down from the heights
           and took hold of me, O God;
           you drew me from the flood waters,
           from all that overpowered me.

A: You brought me into a broad land;
           you saved me because you loved me.

B: You will make my lamp burn bright, O God;
           you will lighten my darkness.

A: With you I can break through any barrier;
           with your help I can scale any wall.

B: How perfect are your ways, O God,
           how dependable your words;
           a shield to all who make you their refuge.

A: You alone are God,
           you alone our defence,
           girding me with strength,
           making the path safe for me.

B: You have given me a shield of salvation;
           have upheld me and trained me with care.
           You have given me freedom for my steps;
           my feet have never slipped.

ALL: GOD LIVES! BLESSED BE MY ROCK.
           PRAISE TO YOU, MY GOD AND SAVIOUR.
           I WILL PRAISE YOU AMONG THE NATIONS.
           I WILL SING PRAISES TO YOUR NAME.

Psalm 19

ALL: THE HEAVENS PROCLAIM THE GLORY OF GOD
             AND THE FIRMAMENT DECLARES YOUR HANDIWORK.

A: Day speaks to day of your story;
             night unto night makes it known.

B: No speech, no word,
             no voice is heard.

A: Yet their message fills the world,
             their news reaches the ends of the earth.

B: High above, you pitched your tent
             for the sun to rest and rise.

A: Like a bridegroom coming out of his chamber,
             like an athlete eager to race:

B: it springs from the edge of the earth
             and runs its course across the sky
             till it reaches the far horizon;
             nothing escapes its heat.

A: Your law, O God, is perfect,
             refreshing the soul.
             Your rule is sure,
             making wise the simple.

B: Your precepts, O God, are right,
             gladdening the heart.
             Your command is clear,
             giving light to the eyes.   ▶

A: Fear of you, O God, is holy,

        enduring for ever.

        Your decrees are faithful,

        and all of them just.

B: They are more to be desired than gold,

        than the purest gold,

        and sweeter than honey

        dripping from the comb.

A: In them is your servant taught;

        observing them brings great reward.

B: But who can discern all their failings?

        From hidden faults forgive me.

A: Restrain me, too, from wilful sins,

        lest they take me over.

ALL: MAY THE WORDS OF MY MOUTH

        AND THE THOUGHTS OF MY HEART

        BE ACCEPTABLE TO YOU,

        O GOD, MY ROCK, MY REDEEMER.

Psalm 22

A: My God, my God, why have you forsaken me?

        Why are you so far from me,

        from my desperate cries for help?

B: I call you by day, O my God,

        but you do not answer me;

        by night, but I find no rest.

A: Yet you are the Holy One,

        praised by the people

        and enthroned in the sanctuary.

B: In you our ancestors put their trust.

        They trusted, and you set them free;

        they cried and were delivered;

        they trusted you, and were not disappointed.

A: But I am a worm, hardly human,

        despised by all, mocked by the crowd.

        All who see me jeer at me.

        They sneer at me, shaking their heads:

B: 'You relied on God; let God help you!

        If God loves you, let God save you!'

A: Yet it was you who drew me from the womb

        and soothed me at my mother's breast.

        I have belonged to you from my birth;

        from my mother's womb you have been my God.

B: I will tell out your name to my people;

        I will praise you where they are assembled.

A: For you did not despise or disregard

        the poverty of the poor;

        you did not hide your face from me

        but heard when I cried to you.

B: You inspire my praise in the great assembly.

        I will make good my promise before your faithful people. ▶

A: All the ends of the earth will remember
        and turn again to you.
        Families of all races will worship you,
        for you hold dominion over the nations.

B: Even those who sleep in the earth
        will bow before you;
        but how can these, our ancestors,
        serve you from the grave?

A: It is I who must live for you, O God!
        It is my descendants who will serve you;
        the coming generation will be told of you.

B: And they will proclaim your deliverance
        to people yet unborn,
        saying, These things God has done.

ALL: AMEN.

Psalm 23

A: You are my shepherd, O God;
        I need nothing more.

B: You let me lie down in green pastures;
        you lead me beside still waters
        where you revive my spirit.

A: You guide me in the right paths,
        for you are true to your name.

B: Even if I walked through a valley as dark as death

          I would fear no harm;

          for you are at my side.

          Your staff and crook give me courage.

A: You spread a table for me

          under the eyes of my enemies.

          You anoint my head with oil;

          my cup brims over.

B: Goodness and kindness unfailing

          will follow me all my days.

          I shall make my home in the house of God

          for as long as I shall live.

ALL: AMEN.

Psalm 29

A: Give glory to God, you powers of heaven!

          Give glory! Honour God's might!

          Honour the glorious name of God;

          worship in splendour and holiness.

B: The voice of God sounds in the seas,

          echoing over the oceans.

          The powerful voice of God is heard

          in all its splendour and majesty.

A: The voice of God shatters the cedars,

          shatters the cedars of Lebanon;   ▶

makes their mountains skip like calves,
Mount Hermon like young oxen.

B: The voice of God makes lightning flash,
and whirls the sand in the desert.
The desert of Kadesh shudders and writhes
like a hind giving birth to her calf.

A: The voice of God rends the oak trees
and strips the forests bare.
Everyone in the temple
cries, Glory!

B: Enthroned above the flood waters,
God reigns over all and for ever.
Give strength to your people, Almighty God,
and give them your blessing of peace.

ALL: AMEN.

Psalm 30

ALL: SING PRAISE TO GOD, ALL YOU FAITHFUL PEOPLE!
GIVE THANKS TO THE HOLY NAME OF GOD!

A: I cried to you for help, O God,
and you, my God, have healed me.

B: I was on my way to the depths below,
but you have restored my life.

A: The moment of anger
becomes a lifetime of goodness.

B: The tears of night

          turn to joy with the dawn.

A: You have changed my sadness

          to a joyful dance.

B: You have taken away my sorrow

          and surrounded me with joy.

ALL: MY SOUL WILL SING YOUR PRAISE

          AND NEVER BE SILENT.

          O GOD, MY GOD,

          I WILL GIVE YOU THANKS FOR EVER.

Psalm 34

A: I will keep on thanking God

          with constant words of prayer.

B: I will glory in the living God.

          The humble will hear and be glad.

A: Raise your voice with me in praise of God!

          Let all of us together tell out God's holy name!

B: God answers when I pray for help,

          and frees me from my fears.

A: God hears when this poor wretch cries,

          and saves me from my troubles.

B: Gaze upon God

          and your face will grow bright with joy;

          your head will no longer hang in shame.   ▶

A: Taste and see that God is good;
        happy are those who seek such refuge.

B: Tremble before God, you saints;
        those who do so lack nothing.

A: Keep your tongue from evil
        and your lips from telling lies.

B: Turn from evil and do what is good;
        seek and strive for peace.

A: Your eyes are on those who are just, O God;
        your ears are open to their cry.

B: You set your face against those who oppose you;
        you wipe their memory from the earth.

A: When the troubled cry out, you hear
        and save them from their distress.

B: You stay with the broken-hearted;
        you heal the wounded spirit.

A: Good people have to endure great trials,
        but you come to their rescue, O God.

B: You redeem the lives of those who serve you,
        and of all who take refuge in you.

ALL: AMEN.

Psalm 37

A: Do not be anxious because of the wicked
        or envious of those who do wrong,
            for they will wither as quickly as grass
            and fade like the green of the fields.

B: Trust in God and do what is good;
            settle down and be at peace.
        Let your God be your delight
            and grant your heart's desire.

A: Give your life over to God
            to act on your behalf,
            to make your integrity shine forth
            and your justice as bright as noon.

B: Be still before God; wait patiently,
            not envying those who prosper,
            nor fretting at those whose malicious plans
            bring down the needy and poor.

A: Stop your ranting and calm your rage,
            for anger creates further trouble.
        The reign of the wicked will be short-lived;
            the land will belong to the humble.

B: Depart from evil and do what is good:
            live for ever in peace;
        for God is the lover of justice
            and will never abandon the faithful.   ▶

A: I have seen the oppressors triumph,

        towering like cedars of Lebanon.

        When I passed by again, they were gone;

        I searched, but they could not be found.

B: So look for the honest, and look to the righteous;

        the future belongs to the peacemakers.

        God is their help, their deliverer,

        their refuge in times of distress.

ALL: AMEN

Psalm 40

ALL: I WAITED AND WAITED FOR YOU, O GOD!

        NOW AT LAST YOU HAVE BENT DOWN AND HEARD MY CRY.

A: You have lifted me out of the deadly pit,

        out of the mud of the marsh.

B: You have set my feet on a rock

        and steadied my steps.

A: You have put a new song in my mouth, O God:

        a song of praise.

        Many will look on in awe, and put their trust in you.

B: Happy are those who put their trust in God,

        and do not look to the arrogant and the treacherous.

A: God, our God, what wonders you have done for us!

        What plans you have made for us; you have no equal!

B: I would proclaim and speak of all your deeds,
but they are more than I can count.

A: You do not ask for sacrifices and offerings,
but an open ear.

B: You do not ask for holocaust or victim.
Instead, here am I! I have come!

A: In the scroll of the book it stands written
that I should obey your will.

B: I delight to do your will, O my God;
your Law is within my heart.

A: I have always proclaimed your justice in the great assembly.
I will not hold back my words, as you know well, O God.

B: I have never kept your justice hidden within my heart,
but have declared your faithfulness and saving help.

A: I have made no secret of your love and truth
in the great assembly.

ALL: DO NOT WITHHOLD YOUR MERCY FROM ME!
MAY YOUR LOVE AND FAITHFULNESS
KEEP ME SAFE FOR EVER.

Psalm 42

A: As a deer longs for streams of cool water,
so I long for you, O God.

▶

B: I thirst for you, the living God.

        When can I enter your presence?

A: My tears have been my food day and night,

        as people keep asking me, 'Where is your God?'

B: My heart breaks when I remember

        how I went with the crowd to the house of God,

        leading the joyous procession,

        singing and shouting God's praises.

ALL: WHY SHOULD I BE SAD? WHY SHOULD I BE TROUBLED?

        I WILL PUT MY HOPE IN GOD,

        AND ONCE AGAIN I WILL PRAISE

        MY SAVIOUR AND MY GOD.

A: In exile, sunk in despair,

        I shall remember you from the springs of Jordan,

        from the Hermons, from the hill of Mizar.

B: Deep calls to deep in the roar of the waters.

        Your waters of sorrow have swept over me.

A: By day show me your loving-kindness,

        so that by night your song may be with me:

        a prayer to the God of my life.

B: I will say to God, my rock:

        Why have you forgotten me?

        Why must I walk about like a mourner,

        taunted all day long

        as they ask me, 'Where is your God?'

ALL: WHY SHOULD I BE SAD? WHY SHOULD I BE TROUBLED?
          I WILL PUT MY HOPE IN GOD,
          AND ONCE AGAIN I WILL PRAISE
          MY SAVIOUR AND MY GOD.

Psalm 46

ALL: GOD IS OUR REFUGE AND STRENGTH,
          OUR EVER-PRESENT HELP IN DISTRESS.

A: Though the earth trembles,
          and mountains slide into the sea,
          we have no fear.

B: Waters foam and roar,
          and mountains shake at their surging;
          but the God of hosts is with us –
          our stronghold, the God of the faithful people.

A: There is a river
          whose streams give joy to the city of God,
          the holy dwelling of the Most High.

B: God is in its midst; it stands firm.
          God will aid it at the break of day.

A: Even if nations are in chaos, and kingdoms fall,
          God's voice resounds; the earth melts away.

B: God is with us;
          the God of the faithful people is our stronghold.   ▶

A: Come! See the deeds of the Most High,

        the marvellous things God has done on earth;

B: All over the world, God has stopped wars –

        breaking bows, splintering spears,

        burning the shields with fire.

A: Be still! And know that I am God,

        exalted among the nations, exalted upon the earth.

ALL: THE MOST HIGH IS WITH US;

        OUR STRONGHOLD IS THE GOD OF THE FAITHFUL PEOPLE.

Psalm 51

A: Have mercy on me, O God, in your faithful love;

        in your great mercy wipe out my offence.

B: Wash me clean from my guilt

        and purify me from my sin.

        I am well aware of my misdeeds;

        my sin is ever before me.

A: Against you, you alone, have I sinned.

        I have done what is evil

        before your very eyes.

B: You are right to accuse me,

        justified in passing sentence;

        for the causes of my sinfulness

        go back to my earliest years.

A: In my birth and my beginnings
        were the seeds of my distress.
        In the womb, from my conception,
        my brokenness began.

B: You desire deep and inner truth;
        teach me your hidden wisdom.
        Purge me with hyssop till I am clean;
        wash me till I am bright as snow.

A: Create a pure heart in me, O God;
        put a new and right spirit within me.
        Do not drive me away from your presence,
        or remove your spirit of holiness.

B: Restore to me your joyous salvation;
        support me, strengthen my will.
        Then I will teach other sinners your ways,
        that they, too, may turn back to you.

A: Open my lips, O God,
        that my mouth may proclaim your praise.

B: Sacrifices give you no pleasure.
        If I were to bring you a burnt offering
        you would not accept it.

ALL: THE SACRIFICE ACCEPTABLE TO GOD
        IS A BROKEN SPIRIT.
        A BROKEN AND CONTRITE HEART, O GOD,
        YOU WILL NOT DESPISE.

Psalm 63

ALL: O GOD, YOU ARE MY GOD:
           HOW I LONG FOR YOU!

A: My soul thirsts for you, my body pines for you
          like a dry, weary land without water.

B: I gaze upon you in the sanctuary
          to behold your power and glory.

A: Your unchanging love is better than life:
          my lips will speak your praise.

B: And so I will praise you with all of my life:
          I will lift up my hands and call on your name.

A: My soul will feast and be satisfied,
          and my mouth will praise you with joy.

B: For I will call you to mind as I lie in bed,
          and meditate upon you in the watches of the night.

A: My soul clings to you,
          and your right hand upholds me.

ALL: YOU HAVE BEEN MY HELPER, MY JOY:
          I AM SAFE IN THE SHADOW OF YOUR WINGS.

Psalm 65

A: It is right, O God of Zion, that we should praise you,
          that we should keep our promises
          to the One who hears our prayer.

B: All human life comes to you burdened down with sin.

        Guilt too heavy for us! You wipe it all away!

A: Happy are those you invite and welcome to your courts.

        Fill us with the blessings of your house,

        of your holy temple.

B: With awesome deeds, with saving justice,

        you have answered us, O God our saviour.

A: You are the hope of all the world,

        even the distant isles.

B: By your strength you established the mountains,

        for you are clothed in power.

A: You still the roaring seas,

        the roaring of the waves,

        the uproar of the nations.

B: The ends of the earth tremble

        at the sight of your wonders.

        The gateways of morning and evening shout for joy.

A: You care for the earth and water it;

        you fill it with riches, its streams with water;

        you prepare the earth to give grain to its people.

B: You soak the furrows and level the ridges;

        you soften the ground with rain

        and bless the land with growth.

A: You crown the year with riches,

        and all that you touch comes alive: ▶

the untilled pastures yield crops,

the hills are wreathed in joy.

B: The meadows are clothed with sheep

and the valleys decked with grain,

so that with shouts of delight

everything breaks into song.

ALL: AMEN.

Psalm 72

ALL: GIVE TO YOUR LEADERS GOOD JUDGEMENT, O GOD,

AND A SENSE OF WHAT IS RIGHT.

A: May they govern your people with justice

and do right for those who are powerless.

B: May the mountains bring peace for the people,

and the hills bring forth justice.

A: May they defend the poor among the people,

save the children of those who are needy,

and crush the oppressor.

B: May they endure as long as the sun,

like the moon through all generations;

A: like the rains that fall on the early crops,

like the showers that water the earth.

B: May justice flower in their days,

and peace till the moon is no more.

A: May they rule from sea to sea,

          and from the river to the ends of the earth.

B: May they rescue the needy when they cry out,

          and the poor who have no one to help them.

A: May they have pity on the weak and the powerless;

          may they save the lives of the poor.

B: May they redeem them from oppression and violence,

          and regard their blood as precious.

A: To them, long life and continuous prayers

          as, day by day, they are blessed.

B: Let grain be abundant throughout the land,

          and wave on the tops of the mountains.

A   Let the crops blossom like Lebanon

          and the people flourish in the cities

          like the grass of the fields.

B: Blessed be their name for ever;

          may their names last as long as the sun.

          In them let all the nations be blessed;

          and proclaim their happiness.

ALL: BLESSED BE GOD, THE GOD OF THE FAITHFUL PEOPLE,

          WHO ALONE DOES WONDROUS DEEDS.

          BLESSED FOR EVER BE THE GLORIOUS NAME OF GOD.

          MAY THE WHOLE EARTH BE FILLED WITH GOD'S GLORY!

          AMEN! AMEN!

Psalm 82

A: God stands up in the divine assembly
        and gives judgement in the midst of the gods:

B: 'How long will you defend the unjust,
        and favour the cause of the wicked?

A: Defend the poor and the orphaned!
        Render justice to the afflicted and oppressed!

B: Rescue the weak and the poor!
        Set them free from the clutches of the wicked!'

A: But the gods know nothing, understand nothing.
        They wander about in the darkness
        while the world is falling apart.

B: I said, 'I thought of you as gods,
        born of highest heaven;

A: but you will die as any creature,
        and fall like any prince!'

ALL: ARISE, O GOD; JUDGE THE EARTH:
        FOR ALL THE NATIONS ARE YOURS.

Psalm 84

ALL: HOW LOVELY IS YOUR DWELLING PLACE,
        O GOD OF THE MIGHT OF HEAVEN!

A: I pine and faint with longing
         for the courts of the temple of God.

B: My whole being cries out with joy
         to God, the living God.

A: Even the sparrow finds a home
         and the swallow a nest for her brood.

B: She lays her young by your altars,
         O God of heaven, my God.

A: Happy are they who live in your house,
         ever singing your praise.

B: Happy are they whose strength is in you,
         whose hearts are set on pilgrimage.

A: Better to spend a day in your courts
         than a thousand days elsewhere;

B: to stand at the threshold of God's house
         than to live in the homes of the wicked.

A: God is our sun and our shield,
         the giver of glory and grace.

B: No good thing will God withhold
         from those who walk without blame.

ALL: HAPPY ARE THEY WHO TRUST IN YOU,
         O GOD OF THE MIGHT OF HEAVEN!

Psalm 91

A: You who dwell in the shelter of the Most High,
        who live in the shadow of the Almighty:

B: you can say to God: My refuge, my fortress,
        my God in whom I trust.

A: God will rescue you from the hunters' snare
        and save you from deadly plague.

B: God will cover you like a nesting bird
        whose pinions conceal you,
        whose wings give you refuge,
        shielding you, protecting you.

A: You will not fear the terrors of night
        nor the arrow that flies by day;
        the scourges of darkness and noontime.

B: A thousand may fall at your side,
        ten thousand close at hand;
        but you will be safe from harm.

A: God will put angels in charge of you
        to protect you wherever you go.

B: With their hands they will support you
        so your feet will not strike any stone.

A: You will tread on asp and cobra;
        you will trample on serpent and snake.

B: Says God:

          Those who love me I shall deliver;

          I shall raise those who know my name.

A: Those who call on me I shall answer;

          I shall be with them in times of trouble.

B: I shall rescue and give them honour,

          fulfil the years of their lives,

          and show them my salvation.

ALL: AMEN.

Psalm 96

ALL: SING A NEW SONG TO THE MAKER!

          SING TO THE MAKER, YOU LANDS!

A: Sing out to God; bless God's name;

          proclaim God's salvation each day.

B: Tell God's glory among the nations,

          God's marvellous deeds to the peoples.

A: Great is God, deserving of praise,

          the dread of all other gods.

B: Gods of nations are as nothing;

          but the Maker created the heavens.

A: God is surrounded by splendour and might;

          beauty and strength fill the sanctuary.   ▶

B: Give to the Maker, you families of nations,

        give to the Maker glory and power,

        the glory of God's holy name.

A: Bring your gifts to offer to God;

        come to the courts of the temple.

B: Bow down in the splendour of God's holy presence;

        tremble before God, all the earth.

A: Tell the nations that God rules;

        that the earth is firmly established

        and cannot be moved.

B: Tell them that the judgements of God

        are sound, and fair for all.

A: Let the heavens be glad and the earth rejoice!

B: Let the sea and its creatures resound!

A: Let the fields and all that is in them exult!

B: Let the trees of the forest shout for joy

        at the presence and coming of God!

ALL: GOD IS COMING TO RULE THE WORLD;

        TO RENEW THE EARTH;

        TO BRING JUSTICE TO THE NATIONS;

        TO JUDGE THE PEOPLES WITH TRUTH.

Psalm 98

ALL: SING A NEW SONG TO GOD,
WHO HAS DONE WONDERFUL THINGS,
WHOSE RIGHT HAND AND HOLY ARM
HAVE BROUGHT SALVATION.

A: God has made salvation known,
shown justice to the nations,
and remembered the house of the faithful
in truth and love.

B: All the ends of the earth have seen
the saving power of our God.

A: Sing praise to God, all the earth;
ring out your joy.

B: Sing psalms to God with the harp,
with the harp and the sound of music.

A: With trumpets and the sound of the horn
acclaim the mighty God.

B: Let the sea and all within it thunder;
the world and all its peoples.

A: Let the rivers clap their hands
and the mountains ring out their joy
at the presence of the One who comes,
who comes to rule the earth.   ▶

B: God will rule the world with justice
         and the peoples with fairness.

ALL: AMEN.

Psalm 104

ALL: BLESS THE CREATOR, MY SOUL!

A: God my creator, how great you are,
         clothed in glory and majesty,
         wrapped in a robe of light.

B: You have spread out the sky like a tent,
         built your dwelling above the rains.

A: You have made the clouds your chariot,
         you walk on the wings of the wind;
         the storm becomes your herald
         and your servants are bolts of light.

B: You have set the earth in its place
         so that it cannot be moved.
         Like a cloak you wrapped the oceans round it,
         with waters higher than mountains.

A: At your rebuke the seas took flight,
         at the voice of your thunder they fled,
         flowing from mountains and valleys
         to places decreed by you.

B: There you set limits they might not pass,
         lest they return to cover the earth.

A: In the gullies you opened up springs,

            to stream between the hills,

            where wild animals drink from them,

            where wild asses quench their thirst;

B: where birds of the air nest on the banks

            and sing among the leaves.

A: From your dwelling you water the hills

            and the earth drinks its fill of your gift.

B: For cattle you make the grass grow,

            and for people, the plants they need

            to bring forth food from the earth

            and wine to gladden their hearts.

A: How countless are your works, O God;

            all of them made so wisely;

            a world teeming with creatures!

B: All of them look to you

            to give them food in due season.

            You give and they gather;

            you open your hand and they have their fill.

A: Hide your face and they panic,

            withdraw your spirit and they die;

            they return to the dust from which they came.

B: Send forth your spirit and life returns

            renewing the face of the earth.   ▶

ALL: GLORY TO GOD FOR EVER!

MAY GOD REJOICE IN CREATION!

I WILL SING TO GOD ALL MY LIFE,

MAKE MUSIC TO GOD AS LONG AS I LIVE!

BLESS THE CREATOR, MY SOUL!

Psalm 111

ALL: ALLELUIA! PRAISE BE TO GOD!

A: I will thank God with all my heart
in the company of good people
and in their congregation.

B: How great are the wonders that God performs:
a delight to contemplate.

A: How majestic and glorious the work of God,
whose goodness stands for ever.

B: How good to remember God's marvellous deeds,
God's acts of mercy and kindness:

A: providing food for the faithful;
upholding the Covenant;
establishing their heritage amongst the nations.

B: How faithful, how just, are the works of God's hands;
how trustworthy all God's commands:

A: each law in its place, valid for ever,
accomplished with faith and with truth.

B: With an eternal covenant
         God has redeemed the people.

A: With an unbreakable promise and bond
         God has restored their freedom.

B: Holy is God, the Almighty;
         to be feared and held in awe.

A: The fear of God is the beginning of wisdom,
         the pathway to true understanding.

ALL: PRAISE BE TO GOD FOR EVER.

Psalm 119

A: Though the powerful oppress me without any cause,
         my heart bows to your words alone.

B: I take delight in your promise, O God,
         like someone who gathers rich treasure.

A: Falsehood I hate and detest,
         but I love your law.

B: Seven times a day
         I praise you for your just decrees.

A: Peace is the reward of those who love your law;
         nothing can make them stumble.

B: I keep your precepts and commands,
         for my whole life is open before you.   ▶

A: Let my cry reach you, O God;
          that I may understand your word.

B: Let my pleading reach you;
          that I may be saved by your promise.

A: Let my lips proclaim your praise,
          because you teach me your statutes.

B: Let my tongue sing your praises,
          for your commandments are justice itself.

A: Let your hand be ready to help me,
          for I have chosen your precepts.

B: I long for your salvation, O God:
          your law is my delight.

A: Let me live to praise you;
          let your decrees be my help.

B: I have strayed like a lost sheep,
          but I have not forgotten your commands.
          Come, seek out your servant.

ALL: AMEN.

Psalm 121

A: I lift my eyes to the hills;
          from where will my help come?

B: My help comes from the Great God
          who made heaven and earth.

A: God will not let you fall:

        the One who watches over you is wide awake.

B: The Protector of God's people never sleeps.

A: God has you in safe keeping

        and stays by your side.

B: The sun shall not strike you by day,

        nor the moon harm you by night.

A: God will protect you from all evil

        and will cherish your life.

B: God will keep watch over your going out

        and your coming in,

        now and for ever.

ALL: AMEN.

Psalm 126

A: When God restored us to freedom

        it was like a dream!

B: Our mouths were filled with laughter.

        Our tongues sang out our joy.

A: Then they said among the nations,

        'God has done great things for them!'

B: Yes, God has done great things for us,

        and we are overjoyed.   ▶

A: Lead us back to our home, O God,

        like streams to a thirsty land.

        Let those who wept as they sowed their seed

        gather a harvest of joy.

B: Those who went out weeping

        carrying seed to be sown

        will go back home full of song,

        holding their harvest high.

ALL: AMEN.

Psalm 130

A: Out of the depths I cry to you, O God.

        Hear my voice!

B: Let your ears be attentive

        to my cry for mercy.

A: If you, O God, mark our guilt,

        who can stand?

B: But with you is forgiveness;

        and for this we revere you.

A: I trust in you, O God,

        my soul trusts in your word.

B: My soul waits for you, O God,

        more than sentinels wait for the morning.

        Like those who wait for the morning,

        let your people wait for you.

A: For with you is unfailing love
          and plentiful redemption.

B: You will redeem your people
          from all their iniquities.

ALL: AMEN.

Psalm 133

ALL: HOW GOOD IT IS, HOW PLEASANT,
          FOR GOD'S PEOPLE TO LIVE IN UNITY.

A: It is like the precious oil
          running down from Aaron's head and beard,
          down to the collar of his robes.

B: It is like the dew on Mount Hermon
          falling on the hills of Zion.
          For there God has promised a blessing:
          life that never ends.

ALL: AMEN.

Psalm 138

A: I will thank you, O God, with all my heart;
          I will sing praise to you before the angels.
          I will worship at your holy temple.

B: I will give thanks to your name
          because of your love and faithfulness;
          for you have made your name and your word
          supreme over all things.   ▶

A: You answered me when I called to you;

         you built up strength within me.

B: All the rulers of the earth will praise you, O God,

         because they have heard your promises.

A: They will sing about your ways,

         for great is your glory, O God.

B: Even though you are exalted,

         you care for the lowly;

         the proud cannot hide from you.

A: Even when I am surrounded by troubles,

         you keep me safe;

         you protect me from the rage of my enemies

         and save me by your power.

B: You will fulfil your purpose for me;

         your faithful love endures for ever, O God.

         Complete the work that you have begun.

ALL: AMEN.

Psalm 139

A: O God, you search me and know me.

         You know my being and my doing.

         From far off, you read my inmost thoughts.

B: You know the journeys that I take

         and the places where I rest.

You know the meaning of my words before I speak.

A: You are familiar with all my ways;

        you are around me, on every side,

        holding and protecting with your power.

B: Your knowledge of me is too wonderful,

        too high for me to reach.

A: Where could I escape from you?

        Where could I flee your presence?

B: If I climb to the heavens, you are there.

        You are there if I lie in the grave.

A: If I fly off into the sunrise,

        or dwell beyond the western sea,

        even there your hand will lead me,

        even there you hold me fast.

B: If I ask the darkness to hide me,

        and the daylight to turn into night,

        the darkness is not dark to you,

        for night is as clear as day.

A: Search me, O God, and know my heart,

        test me, and know my thoughts.

B: See that I do not follow wrong paths,

        and guide me in the everlasting way.

ALL: AMEN.

Psalm 142

A: With all my voice I cry to you, God;
        with all my voice I entreat you.

B: I pour out my complaint before you;
        I tell you all my distress.

A: When my spirit faints within me,
        you, O God, know my path.
        On the way where I shall walk
        they have hidden a snare to trap me.

B: I look on my right and see:
        there is no one who takes my part.
        I have lost all means of escape,
        there is no one who cares for my life.

A: I cry to you, O God,
        I have said: You are my refuge,
        all I have in the land of the living.

B: Listen, then, to my cry,
        for I am in the depths of distress.
        Rescue me from those who pursue me,
        for they are too strong for me.

A: Bring my soul out of this prison,
        and then I shall praise your name.
        Around me the just will gather
        because of your goodness to me.

ALL: AMEN.

Psalm 145

ALL: O GOD, MY GOD,

MIGHTY AND MAJESTIC.

I WILL PRAISE YOU TO THE HEIGHTS,

I WILL BLESS YOUR NAME FOR EVER.

A: I will bless you every day

and praise your name for ever.

B: Great are you, O God, and greatly to be praised;

your greatness is beyond all measure.

A: Age to age will praise your works

and proclaim your mighty deeds.

B: I will meditate on your splendour and glory;

I will ponder the story of your wonders.

A: People will speak of your awesome power,

and I shall tell of your greatness.

B: They will recall your abundant goodness;

age to age will ring out your justice.

A: You are gracious and compassionate,

patient and ever faithful.

B: Your compassion rests on every creature;

how good you are to all.

A: Let your creatures thank you, God,

and your loyal servants bless you.   ▶

B: Let them speak of your glorious reign,

          and declare your power, O God.

A: Let them make known to the whole human race

          the glory and might of your reign.

B: Yours is an everlasting dominion;

          your rule lasts for all generations.

A: You are just in all your ways;

          and gracious in all your deeds.

B: You are close to all who call on you,

          who call on you from their heart.

ALL: LET MY MOUTH SPEAK OUT YOUR PRAISE, O GOD;

          LET ALL PEOPLE, ALL CREATURES

          BLESS YOUR HOLY NAME

          NOW AND FOR EVER.

Psalm 146

ALL: ALLELUIA!

          GIVE PRAISE TO THE HOLY ONE!

          PRAISE GOD, O MY SOUL.

          I WILL PRAISE THE MAKER AS LONG AS I LIVE;

          I WILL SING TO GOD ALL MY LIFE.

A: Put no trust in earthly rulers;

          human beings cannot save you.

          They breathe their last and return to dust,

          and their plans come to nothing.

B: Happy those whose help is the God of Jacob,

            whose hope is in the Maker, their God,

            the God of heaven and earth and sea

            and all that is in them.

A: It is God who keeps faith for ever,

            who secures justice for the oppressed

            and feeds the hungry.

B: It is God who sets the captives free,

            who restores the sight of the blind,

            who raises up those that were bowed down,

            and loves the just.

A: It is God who protects the stranger,

            who sustains the widow and orphan,

            and thwarts the wicked.

ALL: THE MAKER WILL REIGN FOR EVER,

            OUR GOD THROUGH ALL GENERATIONS.

            GIVE PRAISE TO THE HOLY ONE.

            ALLELUIA!

Psalm 148

ALL: PRAISE GOD!

            SHOUT YOUR PRAISES FROM THE HEAVENS.

            SHOUT THEM FROM THE HEIGHTS.

A: Sing praises, all you angels,

            all you heavenly beings.   ▶

B: Sing praises, sun and moon,
          and all you glittering stars.

A: Praise God, you highest heavens,
          you waters above the heavens.

B: Praise the holy name
          of the God who called you forth,
          who established you for ever and ever
          by a decree that will never change.

A: Shout your praises, all the earth,
          you sea monsters and all depths.

B: Fire and hail, snow and frost,
          storm winds, fulfilling God's word.

A: You mountains and all you hills,
          you orchards and every cedar.

B: You beasts, both wild and tame;
          creeping reptiles, flying birds.

A: Monarchs of earth and all people
          rulers and judges of every land.

B: Women and men alike,
          young and old together.

A: Praise the holy name,
          the name beyond all names.

B: God's splendour above the earth,

          above the heavens,

          giving strength and hope to the people.

ALL: GOD BE PRAISED BY ALL THE FAITHFUL PEOPLE,

          BY PEOPLE CLOSE TO GOD!

          ALLELUIA!

INDEX

Responses

Prayers

Songs

Psalms

ACKNOWLEDGEMENTS

The Iona Community gratefully acknowledges the permission granted to use the following non-Community items included in the book which are copyright as described below. The Iona Community has attempted to contact the owners of all material which is copyright. We would be glad to have any omissions brought to our attention.

'In the midst of hunger and war' (p74) Attributed to Edmund Jones. Reproduced by permission of Stainer & Bell Ltd.

A Christian Aid Affirmation (p81) was created to accompany Christian Aid's Statement of Faith, and is used by permission.

Affirmation from South Africa (p82): adapted extract from presentation by Allan A. Boesak to WCC VI Assembly on the theme Jesus Christ, the Life of the World. In 'Gathered for Life: Official Report', WCC VI Assembly, Vancouver, Canada 1983. Ed. David Gill, copyright 1983 WCC Publications, WCC Geneva.

'Spirit of truth and judgement' (p85), 'Spirit of integrity' (p85) and 'May the God who shakes' (p86) are © Janet Morley and are used with the author's permission. They originally apeared in *All Desires Known* (Movement for the Ordination of Women, and Women in Theology, 1988; SPCK, 1992).

'We believe in God: who has created and is creating ...' (p101): *A New Creed*, used by permission of the United Church of Canada.

The song *Welcome to the Feast* (p131) was written by Janet Nightingale to celebrate the 50th Anniversary of Christian Aid.

All the other material is either traditional or original to the Iona Community, to which application must be made in writing in the first instance if it is desired that such material be reproduced commercially.

Apply to:

The Copyright Manager, Wild Goose Publications,
Fourth Floor, Savoy House, 140 Sauchiehall Street,
Glasgow G2 3DH, UK

Permission to reproduce any part of this work in Australia or New Zealand should be sought from Willow Connection Pty Ltd,
Unit 4A, 3-9 Kenneth Road, Manly Vale, NSW 2093, Australia

CONTACTING THE IONA COMMUNITY

The Abbey, Iona, Argyll PA76 6SN

Tel. 01681 700404 Fax 01681 700460

e-mail: ionacomm@iona.org.uk

The MacLeod Centre, Iona, Argyll PA76 6SN

Tel. 01681 700404   Fax 01681 700460

e-mail: ionacomm@iona.org.uk

Camas Centre, Bunessan, Mull PA67 6DX

Tel. 01681 700367 (Booking enquiries Tel. 01681 700404)

The Iona Community, Fourth Floor, Savoy House,

140 Sauchiehall Street, Glasgow G2 3DH, UK

Tel. 0141 332 6343   Fax 0141 332 1090

e-mail: ionacomm@gla.iona.org.uk

Song sources and copyright

P33 Jesus calls us:
Words: John L. Bell & Graham Maule. Music: Lewis folk melody. © WGRG Iona Community. Published in: CG 66, LFB, SGP 54

P34 Women and men as God intended:
Words: JLB. Music: Kom nu met zang, Netherlands traditional, arr. JLB. © WGRG Iona Community. Published in: OITB

P35 Come, Host of heaven:
Words: JLB & GM. Music: St Columba (Irish traditional). © WGRG Iona Community. Published in: LFB

P40 The hand of heaven (We who live by sound and symbol):
Words: JLB & GM. Music: Chartres (French traditional). © WGRG Iona Community. Published in: LFB

P41 Come, Lord, be our guest:
Words: JLB & GM. Music: Dietwein (JLB). © WGRG Iona Community. Published in: LFB

P43 Among us and before us:
Words: JLB & GM. Music: Gatehouse (JLB). © WGRG Iona Community. Published in: LFB

Key

CAYP Come All You People (Wild Goose Publications, 1995)
CG Common Ground (Saint Andrew Press, 1998)
CH The Church Hymnary, 3rd edition (OUP, 1973)
CTSN The Courage to Say No (WGP, 1996)
EOA Enemy of Apathy (WGP, 1988)
GIA Publications, Inc., 7404 S. Mason Ave, Chicago, IL 60638, USA
GM Graham Maule
HSNW Heaven Shall Not Wait (WGP, 1989)
JLB John L. Bell
LFB Love From Below (WGP, 1989)
M&G Many and Great (WGP, 1990)
OITB One Is the Body (WGP, 2002)
SBTL Sent By the Lord (WGP, 1991)
SGP Songs of God's People (OUP, 1988)
TIOAU There Is One Among Us (WGP, 1998)
TTM Take This Moment octavos (GIA, 2000)
WGIR When Grief is Raw (WGP, 1997)
WGRG Wild Goose Resource Group

P45 Sanctus and benedictus (Holy, holy, holy Lord):
Words: Liturgical traditional. Music: From the St Bride setting © JLB. Published in: CAYP, TIOAU, SBTL, M&G

P45 Agnus Dei (Lamb of God, you take away):
Words: Liturgical traditional. Music: From the St Bride setting © JLB. Published in: CAYP, TIOAU, SBTL, M&G

P47 Shout for joy:
Words: JLB & GM. Music: Lansdowne (JLB). © WGRG Iona Community. Published in: LFB

P47 Sisters and brothers, with one voice:
Words: JLB. Music: Vulpius. © WGRG Iona Community. Published in: OITB

P49 We rejoice to be God's chosen:
Words: JLB. Music: Nettleton (traditional). © WGRG Iona Community. Published in: TTM, OITB

P131 Welcome to the feast:
Words © Janet Nightingale, not published elsewhere. Music: Can be sung to Bleanwern, Hyfrodol or Abbot's Leigh.

P190 God's graceful moment:
Words © Kathy Galloway, not published elsewhere. Music: 17th century French carol melody (CH3 577).

P191 Today I awake:
Words: JLB & GM. Music: Slivers of Gold (JLB). © WGRG Iona Community. Published in: CG 133

P192 Oh the life of the world:
Words: Kathy Galloway. Music: Ian Galloway, arr. JLB. Words © Kathy Galloway. Music © Ian Galloway. Arrangement © Panel on Worship. Published in: CG 97, SGP 87

P193 Enemy of apathy:
Words: JLB & GM. Music: Thainaky (JLB). © WGRG Iona Community. Published in: CG 32, EOA

P194 Dance and sing:
Words: JLB & GM (revised). Music: Pulling Bracken (traditional). © WGRG Iona Community. Published in: HSNW

P194 Christ be beside me:
Words: Adapted from 'St Patrick's Breastplate' (8th century) by J. Quinn. Music: Bunessan (Gaelic traditional melody). Published in: SGP 19

P195 Sing for God's glory:
Words © Kathy Galloway. Music: Lobe den Herren, German traditional, arr. JLB. Published in: CG 111

P196 I owe my Lord a morning song:
Words: JLB. Music: Nafziger (JLB). © WGRG Iona Community. Published in: GIA choral series, OITB

P197 Humbly in your sight:
Words: Tumbuka hymn by J. Chirwa, adapted and translated by Tom Colvin. Music: Traditional northern Malawi hymn adapted by Tom Colvin, arr. by JLB. © Hope Publishing Co., 380 S. Main Place, Carol Stream, IL 60188, USA. In UK via Copycare, PO Box 77, Hailsham BN27 3EF. Published in: SGP 46

P197 I will always bless the Lord:
Words: Ps 34/JLB. Music: Talla Crioso (Gaelic traditional). © WGRG Iona Community. Published in: OITB

P198 The God of heaven:
Words: JLB & GM. Music: Ho Ri Ho Ro (Gaelic traditional). © WGRG Iona Community. Published in: OITB

P198 The love of God comes close:
Words: JLB & GM. Music: Melanie (JLB). © WGRG Iona Community. Published in: EOA

P200 Night has fallen:
Words: Malawi evening hymn adapted by Tom Colvin. Music: Malawian melody adapted by Tom Colvin, arr. JLB. © Hope Publishing Co., 380 S. Main Place, Carol Stream, IL 60188, USA. In UK via Copycare, PO Box 77, Hailsham BN27 3EF. Published in: CG 89, SGP 80

P201 Thank you for the night:
Words: JLB. Music: Compliment (JLB). © WGRG Iona Community. Published in: CTSN

P202 Now that evening falls:
Words: JLB. Music: JLB. © WGRG Iona Community. Published in: OITB

P203 Let us stay together for a time:
Words and music © Brian Woodcock, not published elsewhere. Music available as pdf download from www.ionabooks.com or as photocopy from Wild Goose Publications.

P204 Nears the ending of the day:
Words: JLB & GM. Music: Day's Ending (JLB). © WGRG Iona Community. Published in: LFB

P205 Stay with us now:
Words: JLB & GM. Music: Darkness (JLB). © WGRG Iona Community. Published in: WGIR, LFB

P206 When our Lord walked the earth/Gifts of the Spirit:
Words: JLB & GM. Music: Personent Hodie (German traditional). © WGRG Iona Community. Published in: HSNW

P207 There is a line of women:
Words: JLB. Music: Seven Joys of Mary, arr. JLB. © WGRG Iona Community. Published in: OITB

P209 The love of God comes close:
Words: JLB (based on words of George MacLeod). Music: JLB. © WGRG Iona Community. Published in: OITB

Where to find other songs listed in this book

P65-66
All are welcome (Let us build a house where love can dwell): CG 4 (*see key, p268*)
Brother, sister, let me serve you: CG 16
Christ be our light (Longing for light, we wait in darkness): CG 21
Clap your hands all you nations: CG 20, POPPP
Come all you people/Uyai Mose: CG 18, CAYP
Dignity and grace (When I receive the peace of Christ): CG 29
Gather us in (Here in this place new light is streaming): CG 38
Iona Gloria: CG 64
I rejoiced when I heard them say: CG 59
Jubilate, everybody: CG 68, SGP 59
Kindle a flame: HSNW

P78-79
Charity? (Do not offer me your money): LBD
Come now, O Prince of Peace: CG 25, SBTL
Dona Nobis (Give us peace): HSNW
Do not retreat: LBD, BOT
Don't tell me of a faith that fears: L&A, EOA
For the fruits of all creation: CG 34
Freedom is coming: FIC
From each one condemned by birth: WWFIA
Give us light/Jyothi dho: L&A
Goodness is stronger than evil: TIOAU, L&A
Heaven shall not wait: CG 49, HSNW
Heiwa song (See the children born of sorrow): LBD
How can we stand together: L&A

P78-79 contd.

If you believe and I believe: CG 62, SBTL

Inspired by love and anger: CG 63, L&A, HSNW

Jesus Christ is waiting: CG 67, EOA

Kindle a flame: HSNW

Kyrie (Ukraine): CG 69, SGP 61

Kyrie (Ghana): M&G

Liberator Lord (To those whose times are bitter): LBD

Make me a channel of your peace: SGP 76

Oh the earth is the Lord's: CG 96

O Lord hold my hand: traditional, recorded by Sweet Honey in the Rock

O Lord my God: EOA

Our burden is heavy/Unzima: L&A

Key

AOV As One Voice (Willow Connection, Australia, vol.1 1992, vol. 2 1996)

BOT Bread of Tomorrow (SPCK/Christian Aid, 1993)

CAYP Come All You People (Wild Goose Publications, 1995)

CG Common Ground (Saint Andrew Press, 1998)

CTSN The Courage to Say No (WGP, 1996)

EOA Enemy of Apathy (WGP, 1988)

FIC Freedom is Coming (WGP, 1990)

H&S Hymns and Psalms (Methodist Publishing House, 1983)

HSNW Heaven Shall Not Wait (WGP, 1989)

L&A Love and Anger (WGP, 1997)

LBD Love Burning Deep (SPCK, 1993, now out of print*)

LFB Love From Below (WGP, 1989)

M&G Many and Great (WGP, 1990)

MFT Music from Taizé (Geoffrey Chapman/Mowbray, 1991)

OITB One Is the Body (WGP, 2002)

POPPP Psalms of Patience, Protest and Praise (WGP, 1993)

PTC Praying the Catechism (Division for Parish Life of the Evangelical Lutheran Church, Canada)

SBTL Sent By the Lord (WGP, 1991)

SGP Songs of God's People (OUP, 1988)

TIOAU There Is One Among Us (WGP, 1998)

TTM Take This Moment octavos (GIA, 2000)

WE Worshipping Ecumenically (World Council of Churches, 1995)

WGIR When Grief is Raw (WGP, 1997)

WGRG Wild Goose Resource Group

WWFIA Women's Words from Iona Abbey (out of print*)

Listed songs may be obtained as pdf downloads from www.ionabooks.com or as photocopies from Wild Goose Publications.

Over my head: L&A
Poor folk won't always be forgotten: L&A
Sent by the Lord am I: CG 105, SBTL
Senzenina (What have we done?): SBTL
Song for love (Now we sing to praise love's blessing): words available as pdf
download from www.ionabooks.com or as photocopy from WGP. Can be sung
to Ar Hy Y Nos (All Through the Night).
Stand firm: M&G
The Lord is my light: M&G
The love burning deep: LBD
The Spirit is moving in my heart: WWFIA, LBD, PTC
Through our lives and by our prayers: CAYP, HSNW
Till all the jails are empty: CG 132
Touch the earth lightly: CG 134
We will not take what is not ours: L&A

P92-93

As a deer longs for running streams: CG 10
A touching place (Christ's is the world in which we move): CG 1, SGP 21, LFB, WGIR
Be still and know: two versions in TIOAU, WGIR
Bless the Lord my soul: CG 14
God to enfold you: CG 42, L&A
I waited, I waited on the Lord: HSNW
Jesu Christe miserere: MFT vol. 1
Lord, draw near: TIOAU, HSNW
Lord Jesus Christ, lover of all: CG 75, TIOAU, HSNW
Lord of life: CG 76, SGP 73, LFB, WGIR
Lord, we come to ask your healing: CG 78
Love is the touch: CG 80
Mallaig sprinkling song (Spirit of God, come dwell): CG 82
My shepherd is the Lord: POPPP
Nada te turbe: SGP 79
O God, you are my God alone: CG 93, POPPP
Oh the life of the world: CG 97, SGP 87
O Lord hear my prayer: CG 94, SGP 85
Stay with me: MFT vol. 2
Stumbling blocks and stepping stones (Unsure when what was bright turns
dark): LFB
Take this moment: CG 122, LFB
Thirsting for God (Just as a lost and thirsty deer):POPPP
We cannot measure how you heal: CG 138, SGP 112, LFB, WGIR
We lay our broken world: CG 143, SGP 113
Whoever lives beside the Lord: CG 146, POPPP

P103-104

Come take my hand: EOA

I am the vine: LFB

Jesu tawa pano: CG 65, M&G

Lord Jesus Christ (shall I stand still): EOA

Oh, where are you going: HSNW

Sing hey for the carpenter: SGP 23, HSNW

The summons (Will you come and follow me): CG 148 SGP 118, HSNW

Thuma mina: common version in CG 129, SGP 108

When our confidence in God is shaken: CG 145, SGP 116

Yesuve saranam: M&G

P116-117

Alleluia: various

Amen alleluia: TIOAU

Amen siakudumisa: CG 7, M&G

Bread is blessed and broken: CG 17, LFB

Eat this bread: CG 31

God's table (Since the world was young): HSNW

Holy holy: CAYP, TIOAU, SBTL, M&G

Love is the welcome: WWFIA

O give thanks to the Lord: TTM

One bread, one body: CG 98

Put peace into each other's hands: CG 103

Sanna: WE

Song of the supper: EOA

The Lord of all: EOA

These I lay down (before I take the body of my Lord): LFB

We are marching: CG 139, SGP 110, FIC

We come to share our story: GIA Publications

We sing your glory: © Bernadette Farrell, admin. in UK & Ireland by Calamus

P135-136

Abundant life (We cannot own the sunlit sky): CG 2

Blessing and honour: HSNW

Dance and sing: HSNW

For your generous providing: CG 35

From creation's start: SGP 30
I am for you (Before the world began): HSNW
Sing out, earth and skies: GIA choral series
Sing praise to God: LFB
The earth is the Lord's (Lord, your hands): SBTL
The peace of the earth: CG 121, TIOAU
The song is love (What is the song): LFB
You are author and Lord of creation/Sara shriste: M&G

P140
Agios o theos: M&G
Come Holy Spirit: CAYP
Dona nobis pacem in terra: SGP 25, HSNW
Mayenziwe: CG 84, M&G, TIOAU
Your kingdom come, O Lord: M&G

P162-163
Go tell everyone (God's spirit is in my heart): SGP 34
How good it is, what pleasure comes: CG 52
How great thou art: CG 53, SGP 86
Kneels at the feet of his friends/Fill us with your love: SGP 60
Kum ba ya: H&S
Lord God, your love has called us here: SGP 71
O Lord, all the world belongs to you: SGP 84
Says Jesus, come and gather round: CG 23
Seek ye first the kingdom of God: SGP 93
Spirit of God, unseen as the wind: CG 117
The Spirit lives to set us free: SGP 102
When I receive the peace of Christ: CG 29
When I need a neighbour: AOV